THE ENTREPRENEURIAL SPIRIT
learning to unlock value

About The Author

David Rae joined Nottingham Business School in 1996, and through the Centre for Growing Business he runs programmes in entrepeneurship and growth for managers and student entrepreneurs. Alongside this, he actively researches the area of entrepreneurial learning.

He started his career in publishing, moved on to work in government agencies where he was responsible for initiatives on small business support, and escaped to set up and run a successful consulting business specialising in business and management development. He holds a BA in English & History from Bristol University and a MEd in Training and Development from Sheffield University.

He welcomes further contact with people interested in entrepreneurial learning, and may be contacted at david.rae@ntu.ac.uk

THE
ENTREPRENEURIAL SPIRIT
learning to unlock value

David Rae

BLACKHALL
Publishing

This book was typeset by Artwerk for

Blackhall Publishing
26 Eustace Street
Dublin 2
Ireland

e-mail: blackhall@tinet.ie

© David Rae, 1999

ISBN: 1 901657 64 7

A catalogue record for this book is available from the British Library.

Printed in Ireland by
Betaprint Ltd.

Contents

Foreword

Starting a business has been described as an exciting nightmare, which is only suited to those who are not faint hearted, especially when the ambition is to grow the business beyond the immediate needs of income generation for the founder. Growing a business beyond the honeymoon period, or indeed the period when survival is all-important, is even more difficult.

Entrepreneurs, who manage to start and begin to grow their businesses successfully, are rare individuals with the capacity to develop a very clear vision of what they want and to draw people together into effective groups and teams in order to achieve that vision. What is the fire that burns inside? How do they actually form that vision? What are their strategies and tactics for turning ideas into practice? Do they feel the need to control everything and everyone, or do they let go in order to grow?

These questions are universal to many people, but the answers are specific to individuals. David Rae's book captures the essence of the fire that burns within and shows how individuals have channelled their energies through effective learning to turn ideas into business. David has captured the thoughts and feelings of individuals who have been successful. He manages to show that although a fire is needed, the process of entrepreneurship can be learned.

We are delighted to be associated with Blackhall Publishing through the first book in a proposed series of books on business growth, where the authors will never forget that growth is dependent on entrepreneurship. The series will be based on outputs from the BDO Stoy Hayward Centre for Growing Businesses at Nottingham Business School. Guided by our values, we conduct research which can be applied to the important task of growing enterprises.

Professor Shailendra Vyakarnam
Nottingham Business School
www.nbs.ntu.ac.uk/cgb/

Introduction

WHO IS THIS BOOK FOR AND WHAT IS ITS AIM?

This book aims to help you unlock the entrepreneurial ability within yourself. It argues that entrepreneurship is an integral part of the human condition and that each of us has entrepreneurial capability, which we can develop if we choose to do so. The book is, therefore, written for people who see themselves, potentially, as entrepreneurs.

In choosing to begin the journey of self-development, your starting point may be as a student on one of the many courses in entrepreneurship, enterprise or small business. You may be a manager or employee in an organisation and seek new opportunities and direction in your life. You may work within a small business, possibly family-owned, and aspire to make it more successful. You may not have a career direction at present and see the most fulfilling and rewarding route forward as creating your own business.

Whatever your starting point – and it may be none of these – this book aims to help you to develop the intentions, mindset and capabilities which are vital for entrepreneurial success. The message of the book is that people can develop and enhance their entrepreneurial capability through learning, if they want and choose to do so. That does not mean everyone can be as successful as the highest achievers, or that the development of entrepreneurial capabilities can guarantee success. Rather, the book argues that you can make the decision and learn to be entrepreneurial. If you make that choice and want to learn, then this book is for you.

This is above all a book about people, and it centres on the human process of learning. I chose to write the book because, in researching how a number of entrepreneurial people had developed their careers and business ventures, I was inspired by their stories of achievement. I realised that much could be learned about the entrepreneurial experience through personal narrative, in a direct way that is rarely captured and conveyed by conventional academic research. Their life stories are formed of experiences, insights and approaches that illustrate their personal journeys of learning towards achieving successful entrepreneurship. Their contribution to this book is in bringing theory to life – the 'living theory' of entrepreneurship – and I hope in inspiring and helping others to understand how the individual can learn to be entrepreneurial.

Following from this the book has three interrelated themes:

- The concept of entrepreneurship as 'unlocking value'.
- Entrepreneurial development as continual learning.
- The practice of entrepreneurship as 'living theory' which is enacted and owned by entrepreneurial people.

These themes are integrated in three ways: as concepts, through entrepreneurs' narratives and by encouraging you, the reader, to develop your own entrepreneurial understanding and capabilities through practical tools and exercises. In this way the book links together theory, experience and practical application.

It is worth saying, briefly, what this book is not. It is not a purely academic and theoretical book about entrepreneurship – there are many such books, written by more eminent academics than myself. Rather, it develops and draws on relevant theories and concepts and asks the learner to apply them to their own situation. It can, therefore, be read by students alongside more formal academic works. It is not a guide to the functional aspects of starting and running a small business, again other books do this, and whilst it will refer to functional aspects such as strategy, marketing and finance, these are not its primary concern. This book aims to fill an important gap because the human experience of entrepreneurship tends to be missing from both the academic literature and the business textbooks.

Entrepreneurship is the most exciting of all areas of business practice and study. As a career mode it is fulfilling, challenging, rewarding and holds the potential for bringing tremendous advances, at both a personal and a social level for humankind. Entrepreneurship can make the difference between poverty and opportunity, between stagnation and successfully solving problems. At its heart, it is a creative, dynamic process that stimulates personal, social, economic and technological change. The world needs more people to realise their potential as entrepreneurs. Studying the phenomenon of entrepreneurship may be valid; practising it successfully is what counts. That is what this book is about.

Although the book was written with the private sector, profit-oriented entrepreneur as its prime focus, there is growing interest in the field of 'social entrepreneurship' and a number of the approaches developed in the book may well be of value to people in this important area.

A ROUTE MAP OF THE BOOK

The structure of the book follows the journey, the choices and the actions which the aspiring entrepreneur can follow. Chapter 1 focuses on understanding the nature of entrepreneurship and introducing the essential concepts of the book. Chapter 2 explores entrepreneurial learning as a self-discovery process of 'unlocking personal value'. Chapter 3 develops the idea of unlocking the value of external resources to create and exploit opportunities. Chapter 4 is an overview of the entrepreneurial process, considering the links between personal and business objectives and the entrepreneur's role in creating and growing an organisation. Chapters 5-7 each focus on one stage in the entrepreneurial process of entering a venture, growing it and then moving on to fresh opportunities. Finally, Chapter 8 aims to help you recognise and plan how to develop your entrepreneurial career, based on your personal goals, capabilities and resources.

The book, therefore, combines three essential ingredients.

- Sound, usable concepts which form a theory of entrepreneurship.
- Narratives from entrepreneurs which describe their experiences, insights and learning and provide important insights into the reality of entrepreneurship.
- Practical tools, tasks and assignments which enable you to apply the concepts to your own, unique situation.

Finally, I would like to thank the people whose involvement contributed to this book: the entrepreneurs from whom so much can be learned; Mr John Webster; Mr Tony Leach; my colleagues in the Centre for Growing Businesses and at Nottingham Business School; and my family who have been so patient whilst I wrote the book.

David Rae
June 1999

CHAPTER 1

Some Fundamental Questions

This chapter aims to explore the nature and background of entrepreneurship. The themes which the chapter will explore include:

- What (or who) is an entrepreneur?
- The phenomenon of entrepreneurship in history.
- How do people become entrepreneurs: are they born, made or 'want to be'?
- The concept of entrepreneurship as 'unlocking value'.

Finally, you as the reader will then be encouraged to explore this in a personal sense by asking the question: 'Do I want to be entrepreneurial?'

The term 'entrepreneur' has attained near-mythical status for over a century. The exploits and economic effects of entrepreneurs have been, alternatively, celebrated and reviled by economists and politicians of differing persuasions. The result has been to elevate the entrepreneur into a beast (once likened to the 'heffalump') which is not only hard to define, but also surprisingly difficult to find.

In interviewing people during the research which contributed to this book, comparatively few described themselves as entrepreneurs. They excelled in their fields of technical and business prowess, they had achieved significant success through means other than pure chance, but most of them – and it seems many others – would not readily identify themselves as entrepreneurs. Yet it is beyond doubt that they had all acted – and continue to act – in entrepreneurial ways.

We often apply convenient descriptions or labels to people in business roles: apart from 'entrepreneur', there is the 'manager', 'leader', 'salesman' and 'investor' for example. These labels get in the way of our understanding. By applying labels, they pre-suppose an approach and a set of behaviours and characteristics, which then lead us to see the person, who is labelled, as being defined by that role. So people are entrepreneurs, or managers, or leaders, but can they be all three? Yet people who are looked upon as entrepreneurs also frequently lead, manage, sell and even invest, just as managers, for example, may act entrepreneurially. So the first question to be addressed in this book is whether the most helpful focus is on entrepreneurs, or on entrepreneurship.

Although it may seem to the reader that we are playing with words here, in this book the focus is on 'the entrepreneurial spirit', the ability to think, behave and work in ways that can be understood as entrepreneurial, rather than on 'the entrepreneur' as a semi-mythical role. Rather than entrepreneurs being regarded as exceptional individuals, we can argue that entrepreneurial behaviour is a learned and endemic aspect of human conduct which has become deeply ingrained.

The question must, therefore, be asked: *'What is an entrepreneur?'*

Exercise

What do you understand by the term 'entrepreneur'? Write it down here. Then read the rest of the chapter before returning to your definition.

_____

_____

_____

_____

_____

_____

_____

It really is important to try to establish in your own mind what the entrepreneurial spirit, the subject of this book, is about. This is not as straightforward as it might seem. To help in this, the above question *'What is an entrepreneur?'* will be addressed from three perspectives.

- **Historically**, how did the entrepreneur emerge in history?
- **Theoretically**, what is the academic understanding of the entrepreneur?
- An **experiential approach** to understanding entrepreneurship.

THE ENTREPRENEUR IN HISTORY

Because our contemporary understanding of entrepreneurship is formed so strongly by the experiences, traditions and stories gained from history, we have to ask how it evolved. How, we might ask, did *homo sapiens* first demonstrate entrepreneurial behaviour? Was it perhaps through a progression from simply killing and eating wild beasts to an early form of barter, exchanging primitive stone tools for meat? People have behaved in ways which we can now recognise as entrepreneurial, since very far back in human experience – certainly long before the term itself was first used. It is, therefore, worth having a brief and highly selective look at how entrepreneurship has developed over time, through different historical contexts. For in the history of mankind, we can identify people who have fundamentally reshaped the understanding and organisation of their societies by creating new economic ventures, which have also been closely associated with or even defined political, social and technological changes in their societies.

FOUR ENTREPRENEURIAL MODES

It can be argued that there are four distinct, but interdependent, modes of human conduct in which we can recognise the development of entrepreneurial behaviour. They have each involved a highly dynamic process of change, driven by people who often acted purely in their own interest, but whose actions have brought about fundamental, discontinuous transformations. Each of them can tell us something about the complex ways in which entrepreneurial behaviour has evolved. They consist of the modes of:

- conquest;
- exploring and trading;
- inventing and producing;
- knowledge.

Although each mode has distinct characteristics, which will be outlined below, they also overlap to form an overarching model of entrepreneurial behaviours. The key characteristics of each mode are summarised as follows.

Conquest

Early societies were marked by the emergence of warrior-kings, who led a tribe or people into becoming a political entity, a kingdom or state, such as in the development in ancient times of the Sumerian cities of Ur and Babylon in Mesopotamia. Kingdoms grew and became successful through raising armies, going to war and defeating other tribes, for example in the conflict between Hittites, Assyrians and Babylonians. Power was gained through vanquishing weaker opponents and the spoils of war, such as treasures and slaves, fuelled the further growth of the victor.

The kingdom was itself an economic unit, an enterprise, a business, which needed to defeat others to survive and to succeed: it was the survival of the fittest. The warrior-king, as a militarily successful leader could bring about prosperity for his citizens through conquest. Within the kingdom, settlements and cities were established in which tradesmen, such as armourers and innkeepers, could flourish as small enterprises. However, the warrior-leader had to raise armies to conquer other tribes, and these expeditions could only be financed by successful previous plunder or by taxing citizens and their enterprises. So the commercial activity was limited, since warfare made inter-state commerce difficult and risky.

The warrior-kings operated as brave military leaders, ruthless and often extremely cruel by modern standards. Alexander the Great is one of the best known and most successful of the warrior-kings. The whole purpose of his kingship was to seize opportunities to enrich and grow his kingdom by conquering and destroying or subjugating others, and in that he may be said to be entrepreneurial. Others, such as Hannibal and Genghis Khan, also established powerful empires through conquest. It was within such empires the conditions for the second mode, exploring and trading, which coexisted with conquest for many centuries, were created.

Exploring and Trading

As states grew, and kings became less disposed to act personally as warrior-chiefs, voyages of exploration took place as a means of discovering new riches. The development of a sophisticated trading economy can be seen as far back as the Phoenicians from 1100BC. The Phoenicians explored and then dominated the Mediterranean as well as building a complex network of trading relationships and settlements on the Atlantic coast of Europe and north and west Africa, which they circumnavigated.

These voyages of exploration had to be resourced, and were financed by the king or by wealthy citizens in the expectation of greater reward. Conquest and plunder or control of new territories and peoples often formed part of the political agenda. However, the principal economic aim was to explore and pioneer new and undiscovered trade routes and resources. In this process of discovery, not only resources but other societies were found with whom trading relationships could be established, especially when they could not be subjugated. The venturer tended to be an explorer first, and a warrior or imperialist second.

Whole civilisations and cities developed around exploring and trading activities. From the Phoenician cities of Tyre and Carthage, to Venice in the 12th century and then Bristol in the 18th century, wealthy trading classes and the concept of the 'merchant venturer' emerged. Marco Polo voyaged to China in 1295 and from his visit interest in trading with the East was re-awakened. The merchants visited and bought from these new sources to sell into known or new markets. Traders found and brought back new and exotic goods – silks, spices, precious metals, plants and slaves. Markets for these goods developed, with high prices and profits available for the right combinations of scarcity, desirability and quality. As trading grew, the need to finance expeditions and buying spurred the growth of banking and capital markets. The first modern bank was founded in Venice in the 12th century as Venice became an entrepôt – a place of exchange – between Asia and Europe.

A great era of exploration took place from the 15th century with voyages, to find a western route across the Atlantic to Asia. Christopher Columbus, John Cabot, Amerigo Vespuzzi and other voyagers, were often geographically mistaken yet succeeded in finding the West Indies, Labrador and North America in their quests.

Exploration yielded knowledge and access to new territories, which provided both sources of supply and markets, hence creating new opportunities for trading. Bartering and trading relationships created the basis for markets to exist between producers and consumers, and for traders to fill the gap. Trading routes and networks of trading stations of different forms emerged, from cities along the Silk Routes from Asia to the trading posts of the Hudson's Bay Company.

Inventing and Producing

There has been a process of discovery-based learning going back as far as Man's accidental discovery of fire and which became recognised as scientific research. It has allowed the development of new materials, processes and products to emerge. Scientific and technological discovery accompanied the era of exploration by providing the technical means to achieve it, and also by harnessing the new resources that were found. The discovery process has frequently enabled people to recognise and exploit innovations. Sometimes, the scientist or inventor himself would be able to develop and exploit the innovation but this is comparatively rare. In most cases, however, the discovery was followed by a period in which it was known about but not exploited successfully.

People emerged who were able to apply new technology to a need and in so doing to create a new venture. The 'industrial revolutions' of the 19th and 20th centuries provide many examples of technology being used to transform processes into much faster or more economical ones (for example Richard Arkwright in developing the spinning frame and introducing the factory system into textile production, in the Bessemer system of steelmaking and in the Pilkington float method of manufacturing glass). The development of railways enabled new industries and new markets to flourish, yet destroyed traditional industries from the stagecoach to the craft brewery. Such figures as Brunel in Britain and Gould in America played formative roles as railroad entrepreneurs.

The transport revolution that they, in part, engendered has, over the 20th century, seen the economies of scale and production technology bring about the development of a 'global economy', with fierce competition and in which constant innovation is necessary for the survival of the enterprise, both in terms of product development and process efficiency. New products move quickly from being premium-priced to being commoditised. The scale of capital required to do this successfully has favoured the larger corporation, which tends towards market domination if not monopoly. There continues to be a counter-trend in the development of new ventures aiming to exploit niches which can be created by technology and market factors.

Knowledge Entrepreneurship

Knowledge has always been important as entrepreneurship has evolved. Early examples of knowledge entrepreneurs could be said to include Galileo and Leonardo da Vinci and even Aristotle. There is a considerable crossover between the modes of inventing and of knowledge. But, as the world economy has developed, we have seen an increasing move away from recognising and valuing tangible artefacts – the spoils of war, Oriental spices and silk, manufactured products, such as textiles and cars – to valuing the intangible in the form of 'know-how', creative work, intelligence, intellectual property, and so on. Computer software, biotechnology, Internet search engines and 'information warehouse' marketing databases are all examples of the recognition of value in knowledge-based businesses.

Such businesses, whose only assets are intellectual property, may experience colossal appreciation in their market value before even bringing a product to market let alone making a profit. Service-based businesses, whose only real asset is the brainpower of their people, are able to flourish in entertainment, media, consulting, business services and many other fields. Knowledge itself is being commoditised by the power of technology and communications systems. In the space of a few years, ownership of the means of production, and even of distribution, has become less important and often less profitable than ownership of essential know-how.

The tremendous acceleration in communications and global knowledge networking creates many new opportunities for business ventures to take advantage of the possibilities they create. Greater personalisation, intuitive knowledge systems, biotechnology and nanotechnology are just some of the knowledge-related trends which are creating significant new opportunities for entrepreneurship in the 21st century. The ability of people to form and run a trans-national, even global, business venture based on their expertise as a 'virtual business' using communications technology is a growing trend. If we project current trends ahead a few years, the characteristics of knowledge-based entrepreneurship seem likely to be the following.

- **Operating in a volatile, unpredictable economic environment**
  As existing businesses, markets and financial structures succeed or fail in adjusting to valuing knowledge, rather than tangible assets, short-run decision making becomes endemic.

- **Working globally**
  Changing patterns of electronic commerce, enabled by the simultaneity of communications and information availability, become independent of national regulation and control and mean that even

'small enterprises' operate globally. The nation-state erodes whilst the capability to form trans-national 'virtual teams' becomes critical.

- **Technological convergence**
  Computer, communications and other technologies fuse together and interrelate, blurring supply chains into networks and enabling new forms of enterprise to be set up very quickly to exploit opportunities and to buy access to the technology they require. Speed in being the first to recognise, or create and exploit, short-duration opportunities will be critical.

- **The individual manages their career as an enterprise**
  As the definitions of 'work' and 'career' change, while 'work' and 'learning' combine, people respond by valuing the development and availability of their skills and knowledge. They look for an instant return on their expertise, which may have uncertain future value, and aim to generate individual wealth to finance education, health care, retirement, etc.

- **Skills of intuiting, creating, synthesising and forethought**
  These will become significant in managing knowledge as the information base grows, updates and outdates with increasing rapidity; how we use knowledge becomes far more valuable than simply possessing it.

So in a highly condensed summary of human history, we can trace the evolution of entrepreneurial behaviour from pure conquest, through the growth of exploring and trading relationships, the rise in importance of technological invention and production, to the contemporary ascendance of knowledge entrepreneurship. The entrepreneur's role in history has been crucial, bringing about tremendous technological and economic changes.

Exercise

1. Think of historical or contemporary figures that you would categorise as:
   - warrior-kings;
   - explorer-traders;
   - inventor-producers;
   - knowledge entrepreneurs.

2. In which category would you prefer to be?
   What factors appeal to you most about this mode?

A BEHAVIOURAL BASIS FOR ENTREPRENEURSHIP?

Each of the four modes of entrepreneurial endeavour described above, show people throughout history promoting a project or a venture with an economic aim in mind – fundamentally to acquire wealth or profit. The Phoenician trader, the 19th century inventor, the warrior-king and the Internet bookseller all had one thing, above all else, in common: their desire to create a profitable enterprise. The pursuit of profit and the willingness to venture for future reward against risks known or unknown is a defining element of entrepreneurial behaviour. However, three other fundamental forms of human social behaviour can also be found within the four modes of entrepreneurship. These are:

- fighting;
- trading;
- discovering and learning.

Fighting

Fighting, springing from the primal need to survive by killing predators and aggressors, is an indisputable part of the human make-up. Aggression and warfare created kingdoms and enabled empires to survive. One entrepreneur explained his business philosophy by remarking that both sport and business are forms of ritualised warfare. Conflict and the competitive instinct is alive and well in seeking victory over the competition, the battlefields being the business marketplace where aggressive marketing is an acknowledged virtue, and the law court where lawyers, like diplomats, carry out warfare by other means.

The competitive instinct and the need for dominance tend to drive entrepreneurs to build powerful and even monopolistic positions, to the extent that at the close of the 20th century three vital industries seem dominated by a triarchy of the 'three Ms': Microsoft over computing, Murdoch over communications media and Monsanto over agricultural genetics. Whilst each of these represent the result of highly successful business-building by those involved, they occupy transient rather than fixed positions. The forces of economic and technological change, and the human ability to come up with something better, will, at some stage, cause each of them to be broken up or supplanted by other enterprises. In just the same way, the industrial titans of the early-20th century, which were once so innovative and entrepreneurial, such as General Motors, Philips and IBM still exist, but as mature, periodically complacent and troubled businesses facing an uncertain future.

Trading

If conflict is one primal human behaviour, trading follows close behind. Man learned that when he could not seize what he wanted by force, he could barter to gain it by exchange for another commodity and that this could provide the basis for a more sustainable relationship. The human urge to get what we want by selling, doing deals, haggling and negotiating to become wealthy (and often powerful) is remarkably strong and deep-seated. The network of business relationships around bargaining and contracting in the process of buying and selling to make money forms the commercial core of the marketplace. People do enjoy the social aspect of business, in which trading can even be seen as a metaphor for the rituals of mating and sex.

Discovering and Learning

If we did not learn, we would never do anything new, nor could we adapt to changing conditions in order to survive. Entrepreneurs are pioneers, breaking new ground and exploring new territory. This process of discovery yields new learning – often accidentally, by serendipity, sometimes purposive. Columbus set out to find the westward route to India and discovered the Caribbean islands instead. Learning, by exploring and paying attention to the possibilities of what is discovered, is often the key to technological advance and to competitive success. Every successful entrepreneur has learned to be successful; they have succeeded because they were able to learn effectively and quickly, and by being able to apply their learning. They were able to use imagination in recognising new possibilities and then find out how to exploit them. Discovery, exploration, emulation and trial-and-error have often proved more effective than theoretical 'book learning' which tends to embody 'what is already known' rather than 'what is yet to be discovered'.

THE DEVELOPMENT OF PERSONAL THEORY

Entrepreneurs, as successful people do, develop through insight and experience their own theories of 'what works'. Here is an extract from a letter written by the inventor Isambard Kingdom Brunel, following the beaching of his ship the *SS Great Britain*:

> One principle of action, which I have always found very successful, is to stick obstinately to one plan (until I believe it wrong) and to devote all my scheming to that one plan and, on the same principle, to stick to one method and push that to the utmost limits before I allow myself to wander into others; to stick to the one point of attack, however defended, and if the force first brought up is not sufficient, to bring ten times as much; but never to try back upon another in the hope of finding it easier.[1]

---

1. Rolt, *Isambard Kingdom Brunel* (1970).

This one extract tells us quite a lot about Brunel's personal theory of getting things done: decide on the best plan and the use all the force required to make it work. If unsuccessful, be absolutely single-minded and apply more force. The metaphor he employs is a military one, of troops storming a stronghold. Yet Brunel had been trained as an engineer and, at nineteen, learned to achieve results as the supervising engineer in the hellish conditions of the Thames tunnel. Early in his career, he always had a number of 'irons in the fire', projects – a bridge, a railway, a harbour – which might come to fruition and develop his reputation and success. He had colossal self-belief and an assurance – learnt from experience – that his designs and plans were right, even when they were of a scale never seen before. He had acute focus and energy to achieve the end result, which may be seen even today in the London to Bristol Railway, his bridges and the *SS Great Britain*.

Brunel (and others cited as examples of entrepreneurial people) was an exceptional and talented person. Most people cannot 'be like Brunel', any more than they can be like Alexander the Great or Marco Polo, but everyone can learn from Brunel's theory of getting things done through being certain he was right and then applying all the force needed until it worked. We can also learn from the personal theories of other entrepreneurs; not to copy them, but to understand why they were successful, and to be inspired by their example.

The conclusion of this brief exploration of history is that entrepreneurial behaviour is endemic in the human condition: it is part of our in-built drive to survive. The inescapable urges to fight and compete, to learn, to trade and to seek wealth, have become highly developed forms of social behaviour from primitive origins. Such people as Alexander the Great, Marco Polo, Galileo, Columbus, Brunel and Henry Ford behaved as outstanding entrepreneurs in their eras even though the term would not have been familiar to them and their approaches might well be unacceptable and unsuccessful now as we move into the 21st century. Entrepreneurship is not a static but a dynamic phenomenon – it continually evolves, creating change whilst rewarding the entrepreneur.

The entrepreneurial spirit cannot be suppressed, even when – as in the former Soviet Union and in Communist China – individual business ventures are illegal and are outlawed by the state. Once the political environment in former Soviet Union and China changed in the late-1980s, people wanted desperately to trade and establish their own enterprises. For even though the political intent of suborning the individual to the collective interest was ruthless, many people's innate entrepreneurial spirit was there, dormant except for covert dealing in Western jeans, for example. The disappearance of the controlled communist economy simply allowed this fundamental urge to reappear.

THEORETICAL DEFINITIONS OF THE ENTREPRENEUR

The term 'entrepreneur' seems to have entered common usage in the English language from around the 15th century and is derived from the French verb 'entreprendre', originally meaning a manager of projects or contracts of any kind, commonly including such things as buildings, expeditions or even entertainments. The meaning of the term 'entrepreneur' has continued to change as economic history has evolved, especially during the 19th and 20th centuries.

In classical economic theory, equilibrium existed in a market where supply matched demand, and thus the margin which allowed a trader to operate profitably was minimised by the operation of the market. Disequilibrium, or a mismatch between supply and demand, was caused either by excess of supply over demand, leading to price-cutting, or insufficient supply leading to scarcity and higher prices. In theory, these mismatches offered temporary opportunities for entrepreneurs to exploit them.

Hebert and Link[2] identified from the literature of economic history twelve themes, each of which contributes a different perspective on the entrepreneur. They distinguished between 'static' descriptions of a fixed role, and 'dynamic' theories, in which the entrepreneur brings about change. It is worth summarising these to see the diverse perspectives that they found.

The entrepreneur is...

Static theories	*Dynamic theories*
The person who supplies financial capital.	A risk-taker.
	An innovator.
A manager or superintendent.	A decision maker.
The owner of an enterprise.	An industrial leader.
An employer of factors of production.	An organiser of economic resources.
	A contractor.
	An arbitrageur (market-maker).
	An allocator of resources.

These definitions emerged from different traditions and schools of economic thought, and there is little consensus between them. Rather they illustrate the diversity of views on *'What is an entrepreneur?'*.

---

1. *The Entrepreneur: Mainstream Virus and Radical Critiques* (1988).

ENTREPRENEURS: INNOVATORS OR TRADERS?

A debate of more than academic significance took place between the theories of Joseph Schumpeter and Israel Kirzner, who were both Austro-Hungarian economists. Schumpeter argued that the entrepreneur engaged in 'creative destruction' of the equilibrium of existing market structures and commercial flows, by innovating and introducing new combinations, such as new products, processes, markets, sources of supply or methods of organisation. In Schumpeter's view, the person was only entrepreneurial when they were engaged in the dynamic process of innovating and disrupting the status quo. Profit, argued Schumpeter, was essentially a by-product.

Kirzner, on the other hand, saw the essence of entrepreneurship as alertness to profit opportunities. Rather than disrupting equilibrium, the entrepreneur identified opportunities in the marketplace which existed because of a mismatch between supply and demand and by seeking to exploit them to bring the market closer to equilibrium. Alertness and profit-seeking were the key characteristics, and Kirzner viewed the entrepreneur much more as an opportunistic trader.

Innovators	*Traders*
Focus on developing new products.	Alert to profit opportunities.
Aim to find and exploit new markets.	Operate in a competitive marketplace, which is governed by price.
Combine existing factors to create something new.	Some people are more astute in spotting opportunities than others.
Apply determination and leadership to cause change.	Will buy at lowest price and sell at highest.
Profit is a by-product.	Risk-takers, motivated by profit.

From this brief summary, do you agree with either stance? Do you think the entrepreneur is primarily an innovator or a trader?

AN EXPERIENTIAL APPROACH TO UNDERSTANDING ENTREPRENEURSHIP

Let us move away from theory and see how the direct experience of the entrepreneur can help us to understand the human dimension and the reality of entrepreneurship. To illustrate this, here is the story of the early career of one highly successful entrepreneur.

Alan M Sugar

Alan Sugar grew up in the East End of London. The family worked long hours for little money and, apart from an uncle who owned a shop, there was no tradition of being self-employed or of running a business. Alan stayed on at school, then worked as a Civil Service clerk and in the statistics office of an iron and steel firm. Aged seventeen and a half, he decided to go into the world of commerce.

I wanted a vehicle and took the first job that offered a car. I became the leading salesman in the London area for a firm supplying tape recorders to radio, electrical and television dealers. But I had the audacity to ask for a pay rise, which was denied, and I left.

The next job was in a family business in which he sold electronic components to retail dealers.

You went and sold, delivered, collected the money, gave a full service – a very good training, you learned to recognise the reluctant payers.

By this time his core strengths of selling in the electronic component and appliance market were being developed. The catalyst, which led him to start on his own, was a record company which was selling off a huge quantity of unfashionable vinyl record titles. They sold well at low prices. Sugar saw the opportunity to buy more to meet the demand he knew was there, and expected to be congratulated for using his initiative to generate an instant £100 profit, but was instead criticised for making insufficient margin.

At 5pm on the Friday evening I told him to stick his job and left!

Alan Sugar had saved £100 from his earnings of £20 a week, and invested this to start his own business. The first purchase was a minivan bought for £50. The balance he spent on electrical components, which he sold to customers he had met previously. At the end of the first week's business there was a gross profit of £60.

In 1968, at the age of 21, Alan Sugar founded Amstrad, which bought low-cost electronic goods manufactured in the Far East and imported them to sell in the UK hobbyist market. As the sources of supply and potential markets expanded, the company grew into hi-fi, video, wordprocessing and computers – the company dominated the UK home computer market in the mid-1980s – and satellite television decoders. The business specialised in astute buying, making existing technology available at a budget price to the mass market rather than pioneering the newest technologies.

What interested me most was not being in the same market with the same product as everyone else. So I was innovating and inventing with audio components and being different.

He described the characteristics of an entrepreneur as follows.

Is it born? - Yes it is, but it is not evident to you or people around you. It's sparked off by quick learning and absorption of the environment you're in. The entrepreneurial spirit is looking at and observing market conditions and asking: 'Wouldn't it be a good idea if?' It's something that comes out of people, it's innate. There are academic and technically able people who would never be able to apply what they can do in the real world – it has to be inside you. Having experience and being an opportunist is half way to being an entrepreneur. You exploit an opening, a window of opportunity.

You learn by going and doing it in the real world. It's practical learning, problem solving. Your formal education at school or college will take you so far, after that it's experience. The real test is competing commercially. You need to get experience – as much as possible in the real world before you set up in business. I got on by asking and taking advice from people who'd done it before. Keep the target small at the beginning, do what you're good at, do what you enjoy. A real test is investing your own money – that carries a lot more weight than just having an idea and trying to persuade people to back you.

You have successes and failures – I've had more big successes and a few small failures. You stick to what you know and avoid diversifying. Don't get involved in what you don't know, there are clever people already doing it. We looked at retailing and different distribution channels, but we expanded in areas allied to the business. In Amstrad there's been a product progression, it's always been electronics.

Immediately, Sugar's account illuminates the theoretical debate about innovating and trading. He may seem to be the archetypal trader, in that his business was driven by buying and selling ability, however, he

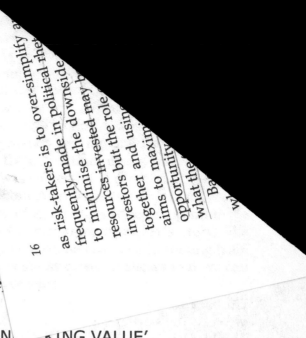

certainly saw himself as
ated demand through o
and cheaply available an
customers wanted fans in
not. Amstrad grew the ma
more powerful players the
ing capabilities enabled it t
but it was more adept at sp
neering new technologies. So
closely intertwined and Amstr

There is another, vital poin
away from the erudite argume
direct experience of the succe
Brunel's is exciting – and he is o
nowhere to establish a successfu
learn from the stories of real entre

as risk-takers is to over-simplify a
frequently made in political rhe
to minimise the downside
resources invested may b
investors but the role
together and usin
aims to maxim
opportunit
what the

16

ENTREPRENEURSHIP AS 'UN⌐⌐KING VALUE'

Three conclusions can be reached from the foregoing discussion, which help to set the agenda for this book.

→ Firstly, entrepreneurship is dynamic rather than static; it does not stand still but changes through time. Static definitions which state what the entrepreneur is, rather than what they do, are unhelpful. Change, uncertainty and exploration of new territory are implicit to an understanding of entrepreneurship. It is not about applying tried and tested solutions to administer known problems, but rather of doing new things, often in new ways. Schumpeter referred to this as 'creative destruction'. Our understanding of what entrepreneurship is and how it works continually changes as people's adaptive learning causes them to behave in new ways, they recognise and adapt to new environments, threats and opportunities.

→ Secondly, entrepreneurship is about opportunity seeking – the entrepreneur aims to find and exploit opportunities which exist or can be created; he seeks to unlock value. Opportunities may lie in what is already known but under-exploited or in the potential of new markets or technologies. Combinations of existing concepts can result in marketable innovations – such as the combined mobile phone, personal organiser and Internet browser.

→ Finally, entrepreurship is about venturing; it involves the investment of resources in order to gain a greater reward. Implicitly there is an element of risk associated with this investment, therefore, entrepreneurship involves balancing risk against reward. However, entrepreneurship is not about risk-taking for its own sake. To describe entrepreneurs

...d misunderstand, an error that is ...oric. Astute operators will always seek ...risk of loss, at least to themselves! The ...contributed by the entrepreneur or by other ...f the entrepreneur is central to finding, bringing ...g the resources successfully. The entrepreneur also ...se the return from the investment and to exploit the ...and resources to the limit, even by refusing to recognise ...limits' are.

...sed on these three concepts, the definition of entrepreneurship, ...ich this book will use, is proposed as:

> *Entrepreneurship is the process of identifying and exploiting opportunities through bringing together resources to form ventures, which create or release value.*

Go back to your definition of *'What is an entrepreneur?'* (which you wrote at the start of this chapter). Do you still agree with it after reading this chapter so far? If not, update it.

A central concept of the book is around 'opportunity', which can be described as sources of unrealised or under-exploited value. These can include the untapped market, the undersold product, the underperforming business, for example. The entrepreneur has a catalytic role in 'unlocking hidden value' and transforming it to release value and to create profit. The 'unlocking value' model, which is shown below, will be explored in the following chapters from different perspectives.

Figure 1.1: Unlocking Value

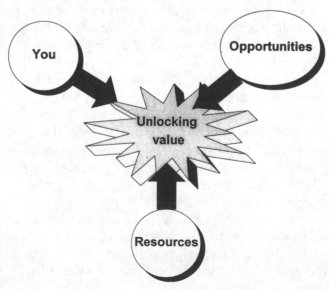

What are the sources of value? The first is you, as the potential entrepreneur. Your value is embodied in your personality, motivation, capabilities and experience. Unlocking personal value is the subject of Chapter 2. Recognising opportunities and exploiting resources to unlock hidden value will feature in Chapter 3. Finally, Chapter 8 focuses on planning how to unlock value from yourself and from opportunities that you recognise.

Exercise

Think of three people you would consider to be highly entrepreneurial under the definition given above. Write their names in the box below. For each of them, write down:

- What was the opportunity they identified?
- How did they exploit it through launching a venture?
- Why were they successful?

Person	The opportunity	The venture	Reasons for their success

WHAT CAN YOU LEARN FROM THEIR SUCCESS IN IDENTIFYING AND EXPLOITING OPPORTUNITIES?

There has been exhaustive research over decades into entrepreneurship, aiming to define the entrepreneur, to find out what kinds of people become entrepreneurs, to examine the personality and backgrounds of entrepreneurs to find common characteristics, traits, and so on. One school of thought proposed that entrepreneurs are recognisably different from other, 'ordinary' people, that entrepreneurs are born rather than made. The results of this were summed up by Gartner in his seminal article "'Who is an entrepreneur?' is the wrong question".[2] His view

---

2. Gartner, "'Who is an Entrepreneur?' is the Wrong Question" *Entrepreneurship Theory and Practice* (1988) Vol. 13, No. 4, pp. 47-67.

was that the study of '*What kind of people are entrepreneurs?*' and the research into entrepreneurial personality traits had failed to prove any shared, common characteristics of entrepreneurs. His conclusion was that the real question was 'What do entrepreneurs *do* to create organisations?'

The starting point of this book is that it has not been proven that entrepreneurs are born genetically or psychologically different, and perhaps never will be. If it were so, there would be a relatively limited pool of entrepreneurial talent on which to draw, and little point in aiming to help 'others' to develop entrepreneurial skills since those 'born' to be entrepreneurs would do it anyway and 'others' would probably fail. On the other hand, we do know that when the economic and cultural environment favours enterprise, more people seek to take advantage of this, to form and grow business ventures. This indicates that there is a good deal of free choice and social learning involved; people, if they choose to and if they want to, can become entrepreneurial. It is self-selection rather than genetic or psychological determination. So this book assumes that entrepreneurial behaviour is learned and can be learned; and that learning may take many forms, certainly it is not just about formal, academic learning. The essential difference is that people 'want to become' entrepreneurial.

This book proposes that entrepreneurship is a way of working, a personal philosophy of values, beliefs, attitudes and a personal theory of 'what works'. It is these qualities that can be identified as 'the entrepreneurial spirit'. Everyone is free to choose whether they wish to learn and adopt this way of working, at any time in their life. Anyone can choose to become enterprising. That is not to say that everyone will be successful. The key differentiating factors will be in their abilities, their capacity to learn, their determination and motivation. Neither will it be easy – yet many people have built successful businesses from starting with nothing, for example entering a new country as an immigrant or refugee with nothing other than 'the clothes they stood up in' together with their motivation and even desperation to succeed. Examples include Andrew Carnegie and Vince Power, the promoter of the 'Mean Fiddler' organisation.

As people, we are constantly in a process of evolving and reshaping our sense of who we are, what we do and where we are going. Watson and Harris[3] have written inspiringly of 'the emergent manager', of people who continually learn through changing, adapting, experimenting and redefining their sense of how they manage. There is no fixed point at which people become 'managers' or indeed 'entrepreneurs', but rather they may become 'managerial' or 'entrepreneurial' in the way they work. The path to entrepreneurial success is not predefined; each

3. Watson & Harris, *The Emergent Manager* (1999).

individual's journey is unique. How then can the individual grow and emerge, developing their own sense of meaning and spirit of entrepreneurship? These are some of the key questions which the aspiring entrepreneur might face.

- How do I develop entrepreneurial values, beliefs and attitudes and practise the skills and behaviours that will enable me to be successful?
- How can I develop a sense of 'my identity', as an entrepreneur, based on and making optimum use of my personality?
- How do I develop my 'personal theory' of what works for me as an entrepreneur?

DO I WANT TO BE ENTREPRENEURIAL?

If you aim to become entrepreneurial, there must be an inner drive to do so. What is your motivation for being entrepreneurial?

The motivation and drive may stem from a sense of 'wanting to achieve'. Many entrepreneurs have a burning need to be successful. They are competitive and feel a compelling urge to succeed, to 'be the best' at whatever they take on. The social trappings of achievement – predominantly being wealthy, accompanied by social standing and power – may also be important. This is the achievement motivation.

The converse of this is experiencing frustration, being blocked and feeling that you could achieve so much more, if only... A fear of being trapped in a career or lifestyle you do not control, which fails to satisfy, motivates you to escape. This is the frustration motivation.

A third motivation is feeling forced by circumstances or pressure from others into starting or running a business, for example experiencing a sense of obligation to take over the family business. Doing so seems like the best or even the only option, but it does not arise from free choice. It is a step taken to serve others' needs or expectations, rather than your own. This is the 'reluctant entrepreneur', which is almost a contradiction in terms.

Exercise

Take a few minutes to identify what factors motivate you.

Tick the numbers in the boxes below which match the statements with which you agree.

1. I want to be successful.
2. I am unfulfilled and want to change my lifestyle.
3. Security is important to me, I prefer to avoid taking risks.
4. I want to be wealthy.
5. I prefer other people to make the decisions.
6. I feel restricted in what I can achieve in my present situation.
7. Starting my own business is a better alternative to being unemployed or poor.
8. I want to form my own business and make it successful.
9. I am content with my present lifestyle.
10. I want to be free to exploit the potential of something which others cannot see.
11. I don't have clear goals or a plan of what I want to achieve.
12. I want to prove to others that I can succeed.
13. I want to be independent.
14. I prefer to accept unsatisfactory situations rather than change them.
15. I am determined to transform my ideas into reality.

Count how many of the statements you agreed with in the boxes below.

Box A 1 4 8 13 15	Total:
Box B 2 6 7 10 12	Total:
Box C 3 5 9 11 14	Total:

In which box do you have the highest number?

Box A   Achievement

These motivations, if they are genuine and deep-seated, are the most positive. It is important that they are what you genuinely want, rather than adopting them because they seem socially desirable. The more strongly you want to achieve these goals, the more likely it is that you will do so. Go and do it.

Box B   **Frustration**

These motivations arise from a sense of being blocked by circumstances or other people. It is natural to feel this way sometimes and to think you could do better on your own. But blaming other people avoids taking personal responsibility. You need to be crystal clear about what it is you really want, and why, and to believe in your own ability and determination to achieve it. You should formulate some positive goals that will give you the satisfaction of achieving them. Frustration needs to be converted into a positive motivation to achieve. Ensure you really are doing it for yourself, rather than to prove to others that you can succeed.

Box C   **Acceptant/Reluctant**

You probably prefer an easy-going lifestyle and to go along with things as they come. This involves accepting that your life is often shaped by forces beyond your control, but avoids having to take the initiative or engage in 'risky' behaviour.

This position is unlikely to produce entrepreneurial drive for achievement. Beware of letting opportunities slip away and of letting others taking advantage. Think about what is really important to you, what you want and all the different ways you could achieve this. Only consider starting or running a business when it feels right and you are totally motivated to do it, since the consequences of failure are probably worse than the situation you are in at present. Alternatively, just go and do what you enjoy.

Before starting Chapter 2, you may want to take a break. Also, there is a 'Skillcheck' questionnaire in Appendix 1, that asks you to assess your entrepreneurial skills. Take fifteen minutes or so to complete it before moving on.

CHAPTER 2

Unlocking Personal Value: Learning to be Entrepreneurial

INTRODUCTION

The aim of this chapter is to develop an understanding of your entrepreneurial potential, based on your past experience, preferred approach to learning, personality and other individual resources. It asks you to look inwardly, to understand and think about how you can best develop your entrepreneurial potential. It encourages introspection and reflection as a way of 'taking stock' of your personal capability. It encourages conscious learning to develop your capabilities further; the more effective we are in learning, the higher our performance is likely to be.

This chapter is very much a 'workbook' in which can you move through a series of questions and exercises which are intended to help you in structuring your concept of entrepreneurship.

Tip
You may find it helps to use a notebook as you work through Chapters 2, 3 and 8 in order to note down your responses to the exercises and questions.

Your prime resource is in understanding the bank of experiences which you have built up so far in life and which you can draw on and use whenever you need them. The aim is to 'make sense of your experiences' and to think about how they can be of most value to you in developing entrepreneurial capability.

Being effective – in entrepreneurship as in any other field – requires an understanding of who we are, what is important to us and why, what we prefer to do and can do, and how we best work at things. By understanding and building on our unique combination of qualities, we can shape an entrepreneurial identity and capability – if we want to. It is about developing and directing our capability rather than trying to make big changes.

A central belief of this book is that entrepreneurship is 'living theory' which can be expressed and understood through personal narratives – life stories. This chapter encourages you to tell your story and through it to reflect on the essential aspects of your own entrepreneurial potential – goals, personality, motivation and capabilities. Understanding your life story is the means of understanding and unlocking personal value.

Figure 2:1: Unlocking Personal Value

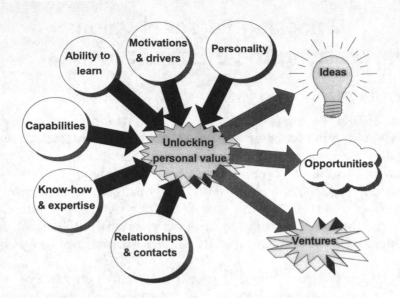

By understanding ourselves, we become more able to unlock our personal value and to maximise the use of our ability. The model of unlocking value centres on our resources: personality, motivations, learning ability, capabilities, knowledge and network of relationships. By having a heightened awareness of these, we become more resourceful and increase our ability to:

- **develop ideas**: to be creative and to make connections which can bring to life new possibilities, products, services;
- **identify opportunities**: to realise ways of applying our abilities and to find potential markets in which to create value;
- **create and manage ventures**: to exploit opportunities.

This chapter explores the potential within ourselves. Chapter 4 will focus on identifying and exploiting external opportunities.

HOW DO YOU LEARN MOST EFFECTIVELY?
What is Learning?

> *A process whereby concepts are derived from and continuously modified by experience…an emergent process whose outcomes represent only historical record not knowledge of the future.*[1]

---

1. Kolb, *Experiential Learning* (1984) p.26.

An information-processing activity in which information about the structure of behaviour and about environmental events is transformed into symbolic representations that serve as guides for action.[2]

This section asks you to reflect on how you learn most effectively.

Exercise

Think of something which happened recently which caused you to learn something new.

- What happened?
- How did the learning take place?
- What did you learn, why was it significant?
- What action or change did it cause you to make?

Experiential Learning

Experiential learning theory connects behaviour (doing), cognition (thinking) and affect (feeling) as a learning process. It was developed by Piaget, Lewin, Kolb, Honey and Mumford. It proposes that we experience real situations, observe and reflect on these, form or modify concepts and theories, and seek to test these in new situations. This is shown in the 'learning loop' model below.

Figure 2.2: The learning loop (Kolb, Honey & Mumford)

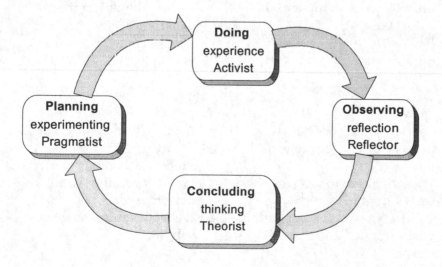

---

2.   Bandura, *A Social Foundation of Thought and Action: A Social Cognitive Theory* (1986) p.51.

The learning loop model suggests that:

- we can learn from experience and use what we have learned;
- we draw conclusions and develop theories from experience and observation;
- all parts of the cycle are necessary for learning to be effective;
- learning must be applied to be tested.

Experiential learning theory simplifies the complex process of learning. It is valid, and can be understood and applied easily to aid our own understanding of how we learn. Although going through all four modes in the loop is necessary for effective learning, people have individual preferences for learning in particular modes. This is, generally, in a combination of two most preferred learning modes identified a 'learning style' with specific characteristics.

Exercise

The table below shows the key characteristics of each of the four learning modes. Which two of these do you feel are closest to your preferred ways of learning?

Activist	**Reflector**
• Gets fully involved in new activities. • Tries everything once. • Thrives on excitement and risk-taking. • Prefers to do rather than think.	• Watches and reflects to understand meanings. • Likes to collect information. • Prefers to think through experiences. • Dislikes being rushed into new activities.
Pragmatist	**Theorist**
• Learns by direct personal involvement in the 'here and now'. • Tries ideas out to see what works in practice. • Values what can be applied. • Open-minded and intuitive learner.	• Aims to find the logic and theory. • Prefers systematic analysis. • Looks for rational and objective concepts. • Enjoys scientific problem-solving.

Which of the four do you feel characterises how you prefer to learn: is there a tendency towards one or two, or a balance across all four? The implication for preferring to learn in a particular style is that we become accustomed and practised at it, but it lessens the effectiveness of our learning overall. So consciously trying to broaden our preferred learning style makes us better learners. Remember that speed of learning is important for entrepreneurial success. Below are some suggestions.

If you have an activist learning preference

Take time to think through new experiences; what happened, how and why? What conclusions can you reach, and how can you apply them? Listen to and observe other people's experiences as well as your own and try to learn from them. Follow projects right through to a successful conclusion, taking responsibility for completing them.

If you have a reflective learning preference

Try to engage in 'hands-on' learning by seizing opportunities as they present themselves. Aim to learn actively, to 'think on your feet' and to find practical ways of using what you have learned.

If you have a theoretical learning preference

Focus on real situations by learning actively, with other people. Look for practical ways of applying theoretical concepts and try to put them into practice. Be prepared to take small risks. Try to avoid dismissing concepts which seem illogical to you but which could have value.

If you have a pragmatic learning preference

Aim to think through 'why and how things happen' to get beyond the superficial 'what works' approach. Take time to reflect, think creatively and theorise. If something does not work at first, persevere, try different approaches and try to find out why.

LEARNING EPISODES

People often find that they learn intensely at specific periods of their lives, although they may be too preoccupied with what is actually going on at the time to be very aware of what they are learning. At periods of change, dislocation and readjustment to new situations, when faced with challenges or problems, significant learning often occurs. These 'life events' or learning episodes are formative in generating conclusions and meanings about 'why things happen', 'what works/does not work', the effects of our behaviour, and so on. This learning process can be readily observed in small children's behaviour, for example through playing.

Idea

Children when playing use their imaginations to create new realities and enact them, practising new behaviours and using things around them in different ways. They have lots of fun and learn a lot. Adults use planning to prepare for the future. It can be dull, limiting, numbers-driven, cerebral.

Can we reinvent playing, and play instead of planning? Use games, imagination, and pretending to create new realities, be totally immersed and act out how we will behave in them?

From earliest life we build up 'mental maps' that embody learning experiences and enable us to access prior learning within our minds. These mental maps include memories of the experiences in symbolic form (the sensory data – sights, sounds, sensations, etc.) as well as the 'meanings' or theories we have developed as a result of those experiences. There are a many factors that can bring about significant learning and change, including success, hardship, challenges, failure, pleasant and unpleasant experiences.

Life events can cause us to re-evaluate our previous learning and to modify or change previous assumptions fundamentally. The learning episode may lead to 'incremental learning' or modification of an existing belief or habit where the new experience updates or refines an existing theory. If, for example, you are running a small shop and find that at the end of the summer trade is slack for a few weeks but that advertising a sale brings in extra business, you will tend to become incrementally more able to promote the sale in a way which boosts the business, through targeted advertising, special offers, and so on. If, however, a major multiple store opens and attracts 75 per cent of your trade, you will find out much more fundamentally about the power of competition and will need to learn very different approaches in order to survive. This is 'transformational learning', where previously used theories and behaviours are replaced by completely new and different ones.

People often structure their life stories around 'learning episodes' – periods of their lives when they experienced significant learning. A way of making sense of learning episodes is to ask the following questions.

• What was happening? What was the context, the situation, the actual events?
• How did I learn, e.g. was it from another person, by experimenting, by discovery?

- What was the conclusion or theory that I developed? What did I learn, why was this significant?
- What action or change in behaviour or thinking (if any) did it lead me to make?

By reflecting on experiences as episodes, we become more aware of what and how we have learned, and as a result our ability to recall learning is likely to be enhanced. Most learning is incidental and informal; it is not planned but 'just happens'. Learning is likely to be more effective if we are aware of the episode – of what and how we learned and why it is significant. Reflecting on episodes also assists the conscious development of a 'personal theory' of why things happen – cause and effect – and what works for us in achieving results.

Exercise

Think of a time in your life when you learned something that has influenced the way you now think or act.

- What actually happened?
- How did you learn?
- What was the meaning? What did you learn? Why was it significant?
- What change in your thinking or actions did the learning lead to?

By being aware of such episodes in our lives we are more aware of how they influence our patterns of thinking and acting as well as of how we can use them. Our life stories are structured around the significant events and phases which have formed them.

ENTREPRENEURSHIP AS SOCIAL LEARNING

Bandura's social learning and cognitive theory[3] has important implications for how we learn complex sets of skills and behaviours. Social cognitive theory is the relationship between three factors (human behaviour, cognition and personal factors) and the external environment. It is important because we do not only learn 'from experience', as might be suggested by the experiential learning theory, but from the complex interactions between the outer world and our inner responses in perceiving, understanding and developing preferred ways of dealing with the outer world. In turn, our perceptions and behaviours shape the world around us.

---

3. Bandura, *Social Foundations of Thought and Action: A Social Cognitive Theory* (1986) p.24.

Figure 2.3: Social cognitive theory (Bandura, 1986)

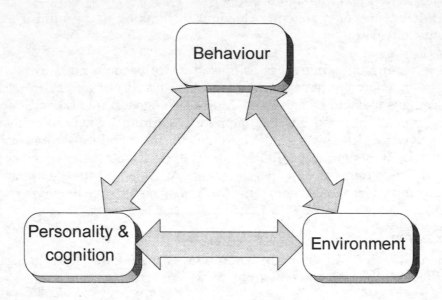

These interconnections stimulate and enable learning. If we imagine a person's first experience of commerce being as a helper on their parents' market stall, their understanding of the personal effectiveness and behaviours needed to be successful would be moulded very heavily by that environment. They would develop a theory of 'what works' and behaviours which would probably be quite different from, for example, a Marks & Spencer management trainee. Bandura identified these five basic and fundamental human capabilities as integral to social learning.

1. **Symbolising**	Understanding and processing experiences as sensory symbols (sounds, sights, etc.).
2. **Forethought**	Planning and thinking ahead.
3. **Vicarious learning**	Learning from others.
4. **Self-regulation**	Developing our own standards and norms.
5. **Self-reflection**	Reflecting on our experiences.

Symbolising

We use symbols to process and give meaning to transient experiences, so that the experience can be retained and integrated in the memory and used as a 'cue' in the future. Symbols are sounds, sights, phrases and sensations which evoke an experience, and can share and communicate it worldwide. For example, businesses create powerful brands that elicit instant consumer recognition and association with a favourable experience. The McDonald's 'M' logo is successfully established as a universal symbol of the McDonald's brand values, and is recognised by children even before they can read. The entrepreneur can be a powerful symbol – to millions of people, Virgin is symbolised by the face and public persona of Richard Branson.

Exercise

How could you use symbolisation? One application is in enhancing your memory by associating symbols with information you need to recall. Another might be in developing a symbol as a logo or brand image for a product or business venture.

Forethought

Forethought enables us to focus on the future, to plan ahead and set goals. It enables us to visualise future situations and to imagine how we will behave and deal with them. It may focus on desirable states – the vision of a successful business, for example – or it may focus on the undesirable, such as the prospect of failure and how to prevent it, but both positive and negative states engender the motivation and capability to act intentionally. The boxer Lennox Lewis spoke about how he trains for his big fights:

> *I usually dream about what I want to happen. I can control what I dream about. It's called visualisation. I kind of run the fight over in my head all the time, things I have to watch out for, reminding myself what I need to do. I dream about winning.*[4]

Exercise

Take a break for a few minutes. Relax, close your eyes, let yourself relax, and imagine a future state you would like to achieve. What would you see, what would you hear, how would it feel?

This is a tremendously powerful thinking tool. Practise using it to develop a personal vision for your life, and your entrepreneurial career.

Vicarious Learning

Much learning can, and does, occur through other people as well as through our own experiences. We pay attention to what they do and the effects of their actions. By observing and reflecting on their actions

---

4. Jim White, *The Guardian* (26 September 1998).

and effectiveness, we can plan how we will act without necessarily experiencing the frustration and failure in learning from first principles. Thus modelling and emulation – learning from experts and role models as well as learning to avoid other people's mistakes – are powerful influences in shaping learning. In the same way, others will learn from us, even without our being aware of it.

Exercise

Think of someone who is, or has been, a powerful source of learning for you. Who were they, what did you learn from them?

Self-regulation

We develop our own internal and personal 'best practice' standards and use these to judge what is or is not acceptable against these norms. Failing to meet our own standards prompts evaluation and motivates us to change our behaviour: learning has taken place. In this way we can learn from what we perceive as 'failure'. Also, we can choose to make changes to our working environment to create favourable conditions for successful achievement, for example by planning working hours, arranging human contact, access to information, and so on. In this way, self-regulation provides a structure for self-organisation.

Exercise

What personal standards do you set for yourself, for example in organising your work? How effective do you think these standards are?

Self-reflection

We have the capacity to be reflective and self-conscious, to review our experiences and the thought processes we use. This enables us to gain a fuller understanding of ourselves and the environment with which we interact. It also enables us to develop generalised theories about ourselves in relation to the external world. We evaluate and update our thoughts and ideas, causing our future courses of action to change.

In being self-reflective, we judge how effective we are in dealing with different situations, and form conclusions about our capabilities and 'self-efficacy'. This is the belief that we can achieve, influence and control events in our lives. It is vital to the entrepreneurial ability to set goals that we believe we can achieve. Self-efficacy is more than knowing 'what to do': it is the ability to form new courses of action for achieving tasks and solving problems, knowing that they will be successful. Self-efficacy enables us to connect the confidence to achieve with the capability to do so.

We make judgements about our self-efficacy based on four types of information.

- **Enactive attainment**: what we have achieved, success and failure.
- **Vicarious experience**: how others perform and the comparative understanding we derive about ourselves. ('I'm cleverer than him.')
- **Verbal persuasion by others that we can or cannot achieve**: this tends to be self-reinforcing, children who are told they are high achievers tend to fulfil the expectation.
- **Physiological state**: how we feel at the time affects our level of performance.

Exercise

What questions do you ask yourself to reflect on to make sense of your experiences? How do you judge your effectiveness? What sources of information do you pay attention to?

TELLING YOUR LIFE STORY

The next section of this chapter is built around your personal narrative. The aim of using this approach is to enable you to uncover your unique experiences and learning, and to interpret and make sense of them. By doing this, you are likely to gain an enhanced understanding of your personal value, and be more able to identify possible ways of using it optimally.

This process of exploring your life story will involve investing 'thinking time' and either talking or writing time – depending on how you decide to approach it. You will need to plan for this – perhaps an hour or so for the next few days. Remember that, as an entrepreneur, your most valuable asset is *always* yourself – so it is worth making time to appreciate your potential value in this way.

Choosing a Format

Much more value will be gained by writing, recording or making notes of your story than simply by thinking and moving on. Here are some ideas for recording your story and insights, in ascending order of technical sophistication – choose the one which works best for you.

- Keep a notebook or 'personal journal' of your life story and use it to record your 'learning episodes'.

- Use graphical techniques, such as mind maps or timelines rather than orthodox written notes (mind mapping is a core technique and some guidelines on its use are included in this section).
- Use a photocopy of the chart in Appendix 2.
- Set up a computer file and key your thoughts into it.
- Speech-record your thoughts into an audio recorder or a voice-recognition computer programme, which will transcribe them for you.

Mind Mapping

Application

A technique for recording information devised by Tony Buzan. Mind mapping has many applications, since through it we can express thoughts and ideas graphically. This gives great flexibility in the way information is expressed and processed. Mind mapping has a range of applications in entrepreneurial learning – some of these include:

- reviewing and making connections between our experiences;
- creating and developing new concepts;
- developing a strategy and plan for a business venture.

Mind mapping works by enabling us to generate thoughts quickly, creatively and intuitively, by 'free association' rather than sticking to a logical process. It can be used by one person, or by a small group – for example to record a brainstorming session.

How to use mind mapping

1. Write or draw the subject in a bubble in the centre of a piece of paper, flipchart or whiteboard.
2. Draw branches out from the centre, label each of these 'who', 'what', 'why', 'when', 'where', 'how' (or use other labels if they are more relevant).
3. Print the ideas/pieces of information on lines going outwards from each branch.
4. Use different colours or simple pictures if this helps.
5. Make connections between associated ideas on different branches.
6. Review the mind map to remove any irrelevant ideas.

Most questions in this chapter can be explored using mind maps, if desired. The figures on pages 24 and 42 in this chapter are examples of mind maps.

Exercise

Think through each of the stages of your life, so far. It may be helpful to structure these as:
- childhood;
- education;
- early adulthood;
- early career, etc., up to the present day.

Take each phase of your life in turn. It may help to take half an hour each day over several days to record your life story. Also, you may find that it helps to think around types of activity at each stage of your life, such as:
- personal interests;
- family;
- education, training;
- projects;
- jobs;
- business ventures;
- activities organised;
- other activities.

For each phase of your life story, choose questions from this list to ask yourself. They are designed to stimulate your reflection.
- What have I done at each time in my life?
- What was important to me?
- What was I trying to achieve?
- What were my successes?
- What were my failures or mistakes?
- Who were the influential figures, and what did I learn from them?
- What did I do, that was in any way enterprising?
- What were the major 'learning episodes' in each stage of my life?

In each of these learning episodes:
- What happened?
- How did I learn?
- What were the 'lessons I learned', the meanings and conclusions I drew from each of these episodes?
- How did I use what you learned, e.g. what actions or changes did it lead you to make?

As you develop your life story, you can interpret it and 'make sense' of it in various different ways. Here are some approaches to sense-making which may help.

Themes

Are there consistent, repeated patterns which emerge – for example in what you were aiming to achieve, what you did, what happened?

Personal Theory

Looking at the conclusions and meanings you drew from your learning episodes, what personal theories emerge from them, about yourself, the world and your ways of working and achieving results?

Motivations

What were the driving forces that motivated you at each stage of your life? Were they consistent, or did they change?

Being Enterprising

Look at the times in your life when you behaved in enterprising ways. For example, in your mid/late teen years, think about anything you did that was enterprising.

- Did you set up any money-making ventures?
  (e.g. car washing, baby-sitting, selling things you made or bought, car boot sales.)
- Did you have any part-time or holiday jobs?
  (e.g. in shops, market, paper round, fast food.)
- Did any school projects involve being entrepreneurial?
  (e.g. Young Enterprise, new product development, business studies.)
- Did you organise any activities?
  (e.g. sports, media, entertainment, travel.)
- Did you develop any new ideas or work on your own projects?
  (e.g. computers, car or bike restoration, fashion, beauty, fitness.)
- Did you break the rules?
- Any other activities not covered above.

CAPABILITIES AND KNOW-HOW

The next stage is to look at the capabilities which you have developed through your experiences and your career to date. These are the skills and knowledge you have and which you can use in entrepreneurial ventures. People tend to develop a cluster of capabilities in their early careers which they build on and use as their 'dependable strengths' – they are capabilities which they know work for them, and which they know they are fully competent, and often expert, in using.

As an example, if you worked in an ice cream shop as a teenager, you would have learnt a range of things in relation to customer relations, cash handling, product handling, hygiene, etc. which are both basic but also fundamental to food retail businesses.

Exercise

Look back over your life story and your learning episodes. Also think about formal education and professional or technical training you have accomplished.

- What are the most important skills I have developed?
- What did I learn which I can now use?
- How can each of these help me, how can I apply it?

As an example, you might see your skills as being.

Skill	*Application*
Social skills	Getting to know people, establishing relationships easily.
Selling	Identifying and relating to customers, selling to them.
Research	Gathering, analysing data to reach logical conclusions.
Management	Able to manage a business, get results through people.
Being creative	Able to imagine new ideas and possibilities.

Now think about your areas of specialist knowledge. These often overlap with skills, resulting in capability and know-how. Don't worry about overlaps – just get everything down at least once!

- What are the areas of specialist or expert knowledge you have?
- How can each of these help you?

For example, areas of knowledge might be:

French speaking	Source products and export sales with France.
Web page authoring	Set up a Web-based business.
Quality assurance	Establish and maintain consistent quality.
Health care	Knowledge of legislation for health care providers.

ASSESSING YOUR ENTREPRENEURIAL CAPABILITIES

In Appendix 1 (on page 189 of this book) there is a 'Skillcheck' self-assessment instrument which asks you to assess your level of skill in the key capabilities needed for launching a venture. It has six clusters of behaviours and skills that cover the following areas.

- Personal organisation.
- Technical capability.
- Interpersonal skills.
- Venture planning.
- Marketing and selling.
- Financial management.

Complete the Skillcheck now, if you have not done so already. It will enable you to assess in which skill areas you have greatest strength, as well as those where you have limitations or weaknesses. It also suggests ways of developing your skills and contributes to the career planning which is featured in Chapter 8.

THE INFLUENCE OF PERSONALITY

Understanding Personality Preferences

There is little firm evidence of a correlation between your personality type and entrepreneurial success. However, by being aware of your personality, you can behave in ways that are more effective. An understanding of personality is important to entrepreneurship because it facilitates understanding of ourselves, of other people and of course the interrelationships between ourselves and others. If we know and are comfortable with 'who we are', our self-confidence and our relationships with others in their roles as customers, investors and employees are much more likely to be productive and profitable.

The study of personality is of course complex, but it is worthwhile. A readily understandable way of exploring personality is through the four dimensions of personality preference which originated from the work of Carl Jung and which have been developed by Briggs and Myers, resulting in the 'Myers-Briggs Type Indicator'.[1] It is recommended that you complete the Indicator and obtain the qualified feedback that is widely available. However, the four personality dimensions are described below and are related to the development of entrepreneurial behaviour.

---

1. Briggs, Myers & McCauley, *Manual: A Guide to the Development and use of the Myers-Briggs Type Indicatior* (1985.)

The Four Personality Dimensions

Jung identified that people have in-built preferences over their:

- focus of attention – the way they relate to the world;
- ways of gathering information – perceiving;
- ways of making choices – judging;
- ways of organising their lives.

These preferences are expressed on four bi-polar constructs or dimensions. People develop a preference for the aspect of personality at one or the other end of each dimension, although both are used and there is no sense in which one is superior to the other. The four personality constructs are summarised below. As you look at each one, think of how on the whole you prefer to behave.

- **Preferred focus of attention and source of energy**

Extroverted ⟷ **Introverted**
Stimulated by outer world   Focus on inner world
of people and events   of thoughts and ideas

- **Preferred ways of gathering information – perceiving**

Sensing ⟷ **Intuition**
Perceive reality primarily   Perceive patterns and
through five senses: factual and relationships: insight,
concrete, 'here and now'   future-thinking

- **Preferred ways of making choices – judging**

Thinking ⟷ **Feeling**
Use rational logic   Decide on relative,
in making decisions   personal values

- **Preferred ways of organising life events**

Judging ⟷ **Perceiving**
Structured, methodical,   Flexible, spontaneous,
ordered lifestyle   open-ended lifestyle

You can, therefore, reflect on whether you are more extraverted or introverted in your source of energy, more sensing or intuitive in gathering information, more geared to thinking or feeling in making choices, and more structured or flexible in organising your life. It is important to emphasise that in everyday life, the behaviours at both ends of each dimension are used, and that both are equally valuable.

The Myers-Briggs scheme produces a four-letter *type* according to your preferences, so that, for example, a person preferring extroversion, sensing, thinking and judging would be described as ESTJ, whereas someone with the opposite preferences of introversion, intuition, feeling and perceiving would be described as INFP. There are sixteen distinct personality *types* and each of these has specific characteristics and qualities, for example in the way they relate to people, situations and stimuli.

The reason for introducing the four personality constructs and the idea of 'types' here is that each of the eight preferences has implications for the ways in which we develop and act entrepreneurially. There are both advantages and disadvantages, or potential strengths and weaknesses, to each preference in the context of becoming entrepreneurial. By understanding what these are, you are able to be aware and build on the strengths whilst compensating for the weaknesses or limitations.

The table below summarises typical strengths and weaknesses of each preference in this context.

Extroversion		Introversion	
Strengths	**Weaknesses**	**Strengths**	**Weaknesses**
• Aware of external stimuli. • Building extensive networks of relationships. • Involved in many things. • Expressive, active learning style.	• Maybe superficially involved in too many things. • Hard to focus in depth on issues. • Less reflective or self-aware. • May find isolation hard. • May act before thinking.	• Focus and intensity of thinking and reflection. • Creates fewer, deep relationships. • Concentrates single-mindedly on one project.	• Harder to build and sustain wide network of relationships. • May tend to think not act. • May find coping with many stimuli stressful. • May be hard to get to know.

Sensing		Intuition	
Strengths	**Weaknesses**	**Strengths**	**Weaknesses**
• Practical thinking and problem solving. • Recognise current needs and opportunities. • Use tried and tested methods • Methodical approach. • Learn from experience. • Value measurable results.	• Short-term view. • May not see, or ignore, future opportunities. • Reluctance to innovate or change. • May overvalue material and tangible symbols of success.	• Sees future opportunities. • Creative, recognising possibilities. • Holistic thinking. • Experimental learning. • Conceptual thinking can produce breakthroughs.	• May ignore current opportunities. • May make incorrect assumptions by leaping to conclusions. • Can miss vital detail. • May waste time on 'what might be' and ignore realities. • May overvalue intangible ideas.

Thinking		Feeling	
Strengths	**Weaknesses**	**Strengths**	**Weaknesses**
• Logical and analytical decision making. • Objectivity means 'hard' choices can be made. • Takes long-term view. • Precise thinker.	• May be critical and negative. • Emotionally disengaged, cold. • May have difficulty relating to others on an emotional level and understanding 'gut feel' decisions.	• Appreciates others and creates empathy. • Strength of personal values drives achievement. • Shapes shared culture.	• May make irrational decisions based on values and sentiment. • Subjective focus. • Resistant to changing decisions.

Judging		Perceiving	
Strengths	**Weaknesses**	**Strengths**	**Weaknesses**
• Planning, organising, deciding. • Creating structures. • Controlling. • Completing tasks. • Time management. • Productivity.	• May over-organise, imposing unnecessary controls and structures. • Inflexible responding to unplanned events. • Finds it hard to 'let go' or delegate.	• Flexible responding to the unexpected. • Curious, investigative. • Values spontaneity, independence. • Gives others freedom.	• May be disorganised. • Ineffective planning. • Dislikes structure and may fail to control vital tasks. • May not complete tasks. • Can waste time.

Exercise
- What do you think the strengths and weaknesses of your own personality preferences may be, in relation to the four dimensions shown above?
- How can you develop and make optimum use of your personality in working entrepreneurially?

Relationships and Contacts

It is often said that 'it's not what you know, it's who you know that counts'. Certainly both are important. Your network of contacts is as significant as your bank of experiences. Your entrepreneurial potential will grow as that network grows.

Exercise
- Take a large piece of paper. Draw a mind map to identify your network of contacts. The branches of the mind map might start off looking like this:

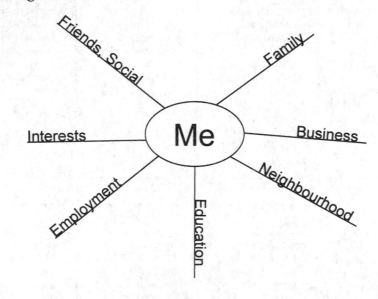

Add the people you know to the branches of the map. You probably have dozens, maybe even hundreds of contacts.

Now review your mind map, and ask the following question.

- How can each of these people help me in an entrepreneurial venture?

Their help might be, for example, as:

- customers;
- investors of capital or lenders;
- able to contribute non-financial resources, e.g. workspace;
- door-openers to other powerful or useful people;
- suppliers;
- advisors;
- partners, co-workers or associates.

There is usually a goodwill factor with people we know. Their help is generally free, up to a point. They will help us to a degree, depending on the depth of the relationship and their view of us. They also have motivations and goals which will affect their degree of support: consider what's in it for them? To maintain the relationship, we need to be prepared to reciprocate, and to help them in some way in the future. Having said all that, it is much easier to get help from people we know than strangers (or 'friends we have not yet met').

SUCCESSFUL ENTREPRENEURIAL LEARNING – A MODEL

This final section of the chapter brings together the essential elements of how people learn and develop entrepreneurial capability in a single, unifying model. This draws on the theories of learning, personality and entrepreneurship, which the book has explored. However, its primary source is the direct research in the interviews with entrepreneurs that form the basis of Chapters 5-7. These elements are shown in Figure 2.4 below which illustrates the development of entrepreneurial capability over time.

Each element is briefly described to explain its significance and connectivity within the whole process. It combines the 'achievement orientation' of setting and achieving goals with the 'learning orientation' of developing and using the capabilities that will enable successful achievement. This is followed by a series of exercises that ask you to relate the elements of entrepreneurial learning to your own development. This brings together all the earlier work you have done within this chapter.

Figure 2.4: The entrepreneurial learning model.

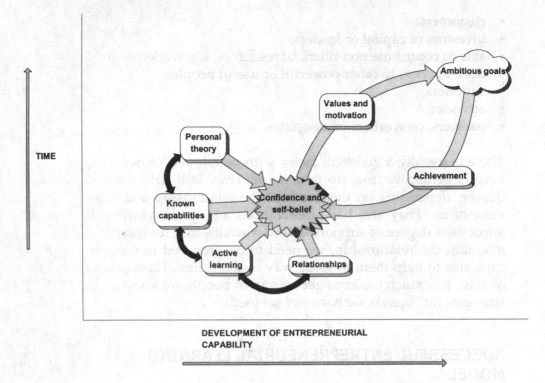

The Process and Key Elements of Entrepreneurial Learning

Ambitious goals

Entrepreneurial people tend to develop a clear set of ambitious goals, which they plan to achieve. In this way they are developing a picture of a future state, a personalised vision which they aim to achieve. The goals are typically career and business oriented, and individuals evolve plans of varying degrees of sophistication and time period around the goals. They work in very focused (even single-minded), goal-directed ways to achieve their goals. This instrumental behaviour also has the effect of structuring learning in a goal-directed way; they learn what they need to do in order to attain the goals.

Values and motivation

There is a high degree of motivation based on a strong need for achievement to achieve the goals. This motivation for self-actualisation engenders persistence, drive and single-mindeness in pursuit of the goal. Motivating factors often include a wish to be wealthy, to be in a powerful, controlling position, to achieve the social recognition of 'having made it' (even to prove to others who doubted their ability and that they could achieve), and to realise personal independence through owning their own business.

Confidence and self-belief

Entrepreneurial people tend to have high levels of self-belief and are confident in their ability to succeed. 'If you believe, you will achieve' is a basic theory-in-use. Self-efficacy is a prime characteristic whilst self-doubt and lack of confidence are rarely a factor, since a positive cycle of achievement together with mental discipline work to overcome doubts about the ability to succeed. Rather the entrepreneur is frequently prepared to challenge themselves by taking on goals which are bigger and tougher; they have learned that they can and will achieve.

Achievement

By achieving goals, entrepreneurs experience a strong sense of fulfilment and the experience confirms their self-concept of being able to achieve what they set out to do. This positive cycle of reinforcement is self-renewing in that accomplishment of one goal motivates the search for and the drive to accomplish the next challenge. In this way there is a powerful sense of a 'personal best' and standards which they aim to achieve or, if possible, improve on.

Active learning

Learning is often highly instrumental, by being goal-oriented. Learning is gained through using a rich variety of sources and methods. However, learning is frequently experiential, concrete and active in nature, being based on experimenting and discovery. Learning occurs and is utilised quickly. Lack of success tends to be reflected on, leading to a change in approach. Earlier in his chapter, the exercises on learning styles should have helped you to understand how you prefer to learn.

Relationships

Significant relationships with others are often important in entrepreneurial learning. People refer to individuals who have (or continue to) inspire them, from whom they learned, and who gave them the initial confidence and impetus at an early stage, entrepreneurs they have worked with and learned from, by observing how they worked, or have been coached by. They have seen others achieve and have decided they could do as well or better. They continue to learn from networks of other entrepreneurs, experts and others. As Chapters 6 and 7 will show, as their capability develops, the entrepreneur becomes increasingly involved in helping others to learn.

Known capabilities

Entrepreneurial people tend to develop a set of core capabilities, generally in the early stages of their career and often in employment before embarking on their own business ventures. Early professional or technical skills, be they in marketing, law, finance, design or engineering, form a set of 'reliable strengths' which they continue to use and develop throughout their careers, and to which a range of other capabilities are added through experience. Through your life story you will have identified your capabilities.

Personal theory

As outlined earlier in this chapter, entrepreneurial people tend to develop personal theories based on the sense they have derived from their learning episodes. Their theories – of what works, how it works and why things happen – centre on working effectively to achieve optimum results and guide their decisions and behaviours. The role of memory is significant in developing and accessing personal theories quickly when needed in relation to a problem or decision. In many situations this becomes an unconscious process – the entrepreneur may not be aware that they are accessing their prior experiences to synthesise a decision or formulate a strategy. At this point they may be said to practising tacit skills – they are working at an intuitive level because from experience they 'know what works' and they do not need to work through the problem consciously. Again, reflecting on your life story should help you become aware of your personal theory.

USING THE ENTREPRENEURIAL LEARNING MODEL

So far in this chapter, we have explored the elements of personal theory, known capabilities, relationships and active learning. Through the exercises you have been encouraged to uncover and make sense of your own qualities in each of these. The elements of confidence and self-belief, values and motivation, and ambitious goals are explored in the final section of this chapter, and complete the model.

You can use the model of entrepreneurial learning to develop your own learning map. Draw it as a mind map and summarise on it your own personal theory, goals, values, capabilities, and so on. This will enable you to review and plan your own entrepreneurial development.

Confidence and Self-belief

- Do you believe you can achieve whatever you set out to do?
- Do you instinctively 'go for it' or do you hesitate?
- Are you doubtful about being able to achieve your goals?
- Do you worry about what others say about you?
- Are you anxious about the prospect of failing?

These questions should get you to think about your level of self-efficacy. Confidence, like many attributes, is one that some people just seem to have, and most of us have to build up. Confidence is acquired through experience of successful performance and by feedback which tells us that we have performed successfully. Think of two speakers at a conference, one being given a standing ovation and the other booed. The effects on their self-confidence can easily be imagined.

Throughout life, the messages we receive from others as well as our 'self-talk' within ourselves are of vital importance. This starts in childhood, when positive reinforcement is essential in building self-confidence. Telling yourself that you *can* achieve a goal is likely to reinforce the belief and the intent to attain it.

The previous sections of this chapter, for example on capabilities, should have helped reinforce your self-belief – you have achieved, and learned, a significant amount. You know what you can do, what your strengths are. However, we can usually achieve more than we think we are capable of. Sometimes 'not knowing it can't be done' is a virtue because people go on to break established dogmas about what is or is not possible. Anything is possible, if we believe it to be so.

Exercise

- Write 1,2,3 beside the top three factors, in the left-hand column, which give you confidence in yourself.
- Write 1,2,3 beside the top three factors, in the right-hand column, which detract from your self-confidence.
- Add your own factors to either column.

Confidence givers	Confidence sappers
• Inner belief that I can achieve. • Successful prior performance. • I visualise the end result. • Positive feedback from others. • I tell myself I can do it. • I am motivated to achieve difficult goals. • I see others succeed. • I start, make progress and this helps me continue. • I don't consider the possibility of failure.	• Self-doubt. • Previous failure to achieve. • Unsure about level of skill. • Critical feedback from others. • I've seen others fail. • Negative self-talk: 'I'm not sure I can do this'. • I fail to complete projects. • Lose nerve at a vital moment. • Frightened of failing.

Confidence is affected by our inner dialogue and by external reinforcement. Which of these affects you most, in positive and negative ways? Here are some ways of building self-belief. Select and use the ways that seem right for you.

- Use the confidence givers. Do more of what builds your confidence. Avoid, ignore or change the confidence-sappers.
- Develop positive self-talk. Praise yourself when you succeed, even in small but significant things.
- Break big, overpowering goals into small tasks, which you can accomplish step by step and cross them off the list.
- Ask someone you trust to give you honest feedback when you are trying to do something new.
- Celebrate other people's successes as well as your own.

VALUES AND MOTIVATION

> *I'll tell you what I want, what I really really want.*
> The Spice Girls

Motivation, values, self-confidence and goal setting are integrally linked. This section involves thinking about our driving, motivating forces. These are in a sense the 'why' we want to achieve. The next section is about goals, the 'what' we want to achieve. In Chapter 1, we discussed achievement, frustration and reluctant motivation. This section is purely about motivation in relation to wanting to achieve. Achievement is itself a motivator in that, having achieved something, it provides positive reinforcement and inspires further achievement.

Exercise
- Write down what for you are the really important motivating forces in your life. Most people have 3-5 driving forces.

They might include some of these:
I want to......
   - be independent, control my own life, career, business;
   - be wealthy;
   - achieve worthwhile goals;
   - be able to develop my own ideas;
   - grow and develop as a person;
   - enjoy life and have a good time;
   - achieve challenging goals;
   - be able to provide for my family;

- be recognised by others as successful;
- help other people;
- be secure;
- [add your own to the list;]

Think about your top motivators.

- Why are they important to you? What is the meaning or value you derive from each of them? If you did not have them, what would you miss most?
- Once you have achieved each one, what will it mean to you, what will it give you?

Now we will go on to think about our goals. Hold on to what you have thought about your motivating forces as these will play a big part in shaping your goals.

SETTING GOALS

Entrepreneurial people have big goals for their lives and careers. Based on the values and driving forces which engender goals, the overall life goals then shape the intermediate goals which act as enabling, stepping stones on the way to the long-term life goals. For several reasons, goals tend not to be fixed, but rather change over time. As goals are accomplished, they tend to be replaced by fresh and different aspirations. We learn as we work towards a goal and the learning process affects the nature of the goal itself. So we may realise that what we thought we wanted will not in fact bring the satisfaction we expected. This gives rise to a change in goal. Alternatively, by discovering more about our capabilities, we may realise that the goal was less ambitious than what we could achieve, leading us to aim higher.

Exercise

Do you have a sense of personal vision for your future?
(If not, try the exercise under 'forethought' earlier in this chapter.)

What are your long-term life goals, for your:

- business and career;
- personal growth and fulfilment;
- family;
- social.

Why are each of the goals so important to you: how do they link to your motivators?

Now review the importance and priority of your goals in relation to each other.

Which goals do you want to achieve first? By what age do you aim to achieve each goal? Some of the goals may be interdependent – are they compatible?

How will you achieve each goal: what is your plan to get there?

What are the intermediate goals you need to achieve in order to build towards each life goal?

Think about the actions you will need to take, the timescales, access to resources and the learning you will need to accomplish each goal.

FINAL EXERCISE

Think back over the exercises and content of this chapter.

If you haven't already started it, develop your own learning map based on the model of entrepreneurial learning. Draw it as a mind map and use it to summarise and review the elements of your own entrepreneurial development.

Chapter 8 will help you to develop a career plan based on the work you have done in this chapter.

CHAPTER 3

Unlocking External Value: Focusing on Real-world Opportunities

INTRODUCTION

The aim of this chapter is to identify how we can learn to create, recognise and exploit opportunities. It is, therefore, about developing an entrepreneurial mindset in understanding the external world, in identifying and evaluating the potential of opportunities, and in forming a strategy for creating or exploiting opportunities.

The chapter focuses on the following key questions. How do I:

- create new opportunities?
- recognise actual opportunities?
- assess the potential of opportunities?
- exploit opportunities?

The learning processes involved in recognising and exploiting opportunities is highly adaptive and experiential. Each of us is constantly perceiving the world around us and deriving learning from it, both at a conscious (explicit) and unconscious (implicit) level. A successful entrepreneur will develop, over time, a set of thinking patterns or personal theories (as described in Chapter 2) which enable him or her to perceive, filter, analyse, decide and act on opportunities more effectively than others.

Imagine yourself walking into an environment that is totally new to you for the first time. It might be a market area in an Asian city, for example. Your sensory systems of vision, hearing, smell, physical touch and even taste are bombarded with thousands of new sensations, of colour, noise, aroma, crowdedness. The conscious learning of this new experience, with its many sensory symbols, is likely to remain available in the memory for many years, perhaps even for life. Imagine now revisiting that same market a number of times. On each visit you would not be as consciously aware of the experience as you were on the first visit. Instead, you would be comparing and updating your latest set of experiences to the pattern formed from the first visit. This would make you more aware of differences between them – the range of goods on offer, the locations of particular traders you had noticed the first time, and so on.

This learning, this appreciation of difference, is more likely to happen at an implicit level, as you form mental patterns and theorise to explain differences between your initial and latest experiences of the market. Why are there fewer fish-sellers, for example? And why do people seem so keen to buy sugar cubes? If you bought in the market every day, or traded in it as a vendor, you would form a sophisticated set of models to use in making judgements about supply, demand, pricing, product acceptability, and so on – you would be aware of market behaviours and trends not apparent to the casual observer. Yet you would be increasingly unaware of having or using those models as they became implicit and intuitive in use.

This chapter suggests that, although each person has and uses their own, individual and different models, there are generic models which can be used to accelerate learning and to structure thinking and decision making in the entrepreneurial process. They arise from the interplay between the real-world marketplace, and the perception, thinking and consequent actions of individual entrepreneurs. They are not new models, but they are generally, if not universally, valid. They relate to five fundamental entrepreneurial functions.

1. Creating new opportunities through innovating.
2. Recognising market and product opportunities.
3. Assessing and deciding on opportunities as investment propositions.
4. Designing and planning ventures to exploit opportunities.
5. Trading.

For each of these functions, this chapter will introduce key concepts and tools, which can be used to understand the situation, to analyse it and to make decisions. These represent simple yet fundamental thinking patterns which can be used, tested, evaluated, built on and integrated at a sophisticated level into your own personal cognitive capability through experiential learning.

In this chapter you will be asked to practice the use of these thinking tools by applying them to an opportunity which could form a potential venture. You may already have one or more ideas for such a venture.

Exercise

Spend a few minutes thinking of ideas for possible ventures. Try brainstorming all the possible uses of one of your capabilities – areas of skill and knowledge – which you identified in Chapter 2. Try this with several capabilities, and do not rule out any possible applications. The feasibility, or otherwise, does not matter it this stage; by the end of the chapter you will have evaluated it much more fully.

1. CREATING NEW OPPORTUNITIES

Unlocking Value

As introduced in Chapters 1 and 2, the entrepreneurial process can be expressed as 'unlocking value'. This chapter focuses on releasing the sources of value on the supply side, and on stimulating and exploiting opportunities on the demand side. The process can be demand-led, by identifying demand – actual or potential – then acting to find supply side resources to meet it. Equally, it may start by locating supply side resources which are under-used find a profitable market for them, or, ideally, by doing both simultaneously.

Figure 3.1: Connecting resources with oppurtunity

We can expand the simple concept to explore in more depth.

- Why people buy? Three types of market opportunity.
- The sources of value.

Why do People Buy?

This touches on the complex area of 'buyer behaviour'. However, we are dealing in simple but fundamental concepts. The entrepreneur needs a very clear understanding of who the target customer is – personal consumers, business or public sector purchasers – what they will buy, and why they will select a product or service as a buying proposition. Below are the key questions, which will be formulated differently for a product which is currently available (such as from an existing supplier), as opposed to a completely new type of product. The questions can be used to structure and develop market research.

Knowing the Customer

- Who is the customer? How can they be defined, e.g. by segmentation?
- What are their characteristics, e.g. age, location, spending power (personal buyers), industry sector, size (business buyers)?
- What are their buying habits? How do they buy? What influencing factors do they notice (e.g. trade press, product reviews, websites, personal letters)?
- Why do they buy a product or service? What is the need or desire that is being satisfied?
- What are their criteria for making the buying decision, e.g. are their priorities speed, value, cost, exclusivity, reliability, quality, ethicality, etc.?
- What is the value of the product to the customer?
- What is the total value of the market?
- Is the size and value of the market likely to grow, be static or decline?

Exercise

How can you research the market for your venture, using these questions as a starting point?

What questions do you need to ask, and how can you find the information?

Products and services can be categorised in many different ways. However, the entrepreneur can envisage the product being offered in one of three ways, which relate to the customer's reason for buying.

- **Uniqueness**: the only source of a product, which is rare or scarce, where the supply is restricted. Specialist expertise, computer software, information and certain products can be controlled in this way and prices can be kept high. There is only one Microsoft, for example.

- **Desirability**: the product is perceived as desirable and highly differentiated from alternatives through features such as innovation, fashion, exclusivity, prestigious branding. It is important to continue to innovate to attract 'early adopting' buyers and to stay ahead of imitating competitors. Sony is an excellent example of a consistent producer of 'desirable' products.

- **Essential**: it is a 'staple item' which fulfils a basic need, e.g. for survival, production, etc. Price levels will fluctuate with supply and demand, and commoditisation will tend to reduce margins over time. However, mandatory items can command high pricing, e.g. 'Year 2000 compliance' computer consultancy in the late-1990s.

Exercise

Why will customers buy your product? Is it:
- unique?
- desirable?
- essential?

Figure 3.2: Unlocking value: a resource map of supply and types of demand

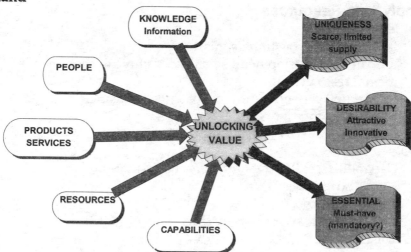

To unlock value, the entrepreneur needs to identify, as specifically as possible, the 'demand' – actual or potential – from the customer (whose needs and characteristics must be defined). The entrepreneur should position the product so that it meets these needs through providing a unique, desirable or essential product. Products, which do not fit any of these categories very well (and these tend to be discretionary-purchase commodities, often lower-cost derivatives of other products), are less likely to be highly profitable over time, although short-term profit making may be achieved through effective trading tactics as shown towards the end of this chapter.

The resources available on the supply side may be in one organisation – but it is more likely that the entrepreneur will need to look across a range of organisations and potential sources. The aim is to identify resources which exist and which are not being exploited to their full value. They may be in use but underperforming (either underused or fully used but yielding less than their potential profit). Alternatively, they may not be in active use at all.

The entrepreneur's task is to identify the resources, to synergise them, to configure them in new ways, and, in doing so, to create new value which meets customers' needs for a unique, a desirable or an essential product. Below is a table showing examples of the types of resources which exist on the supply side and which can be drawn upon. The pace of economic change constantly results in resources becoming available, many of them may be under used or underperforming. They are all available, and can be combined to create new value. It may not even be necessary to buy them – resources may be borrowed, rented, even acquired free. Only two or three resources may need to be combined to create a high-value product, which meets one of the three types of customer demand.

Supply side Resources
Knowledge
- Information on customers, markets.
- Research & development: scientific, technical, economic, environmental research data.
- Intellectual property: designs, patents, licensing.
- Manufacturing rights.

People
- Capabilities, skills, qualifications, accreditation.
- Know-how, expertise.
- Talent, creativity.
- Relationships, access to networks.
- Time, labour.

Products, services
- Underexploited/underperforming products, services.
- Undistributed products in a market.
- Potential for combining/adding value to products.
- Waste products, non/substandard items, parts.

Resources
- Finance: underinvested cash reserves.
- Equipment, plant, road/rail/air/sea vehicles.
- Buildings, premises, property leases.
- Land, planning, development permission.
- Energy, water, air, gases, oils, etc.
- Raw materials.

Capabilities
- Production capacity.
- Technical, specialist or other processes.

- Core competencies.
- Suppliers, partners resources.
- Distributors.

The full resource map of unlocking value therefore looks like this.

Figure 3.3: Unlocking value: the full resource map

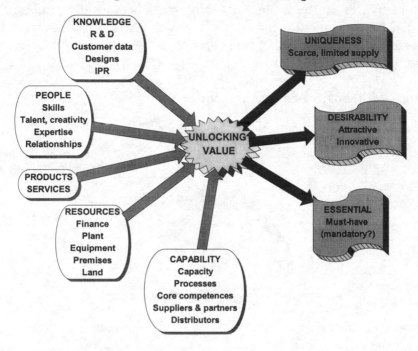

Exercise
- Draw a resource map for your venture.
- What supply side resources do you need for your venture?
- Where are these available, can you locate underused resources?
- How can they be obtained at minimum cost?
- Can resources be configured in new ways to create new product/service propositions?

Creating Opportunities through Innovation

Creative approaches are essential in developing new approaches, products, processes, services and ways of engaging the customer. Technological innovation is often driven forward by people who aim to realise the market potential of technological change. However, good ideas, in themselves, are not enough: and not all ideas are 'good' in the sense of being useful or feasible at the time they are first imagined. They need to be combined with the real-world applications, which are

<u>of</u> value to customers, and there must be ways of realising them successfully. Man dreamed of flying for thousands of years before the first aeroplane flew.

If creativity is the activity of originating new ideas, or linking together existing concepts to develop a new one, then innovation is the successful application of those ideas to market opportunities. Both processes are needed. A third essential is that the innovation can be produced successfully. In this way the essentials of a successful innovation can be envisaged in the way that it combines three elements in a powerful fusion: the creative concept, the value-adding application and the technical possibility.

Figure 3.4: Elements of successful innovation

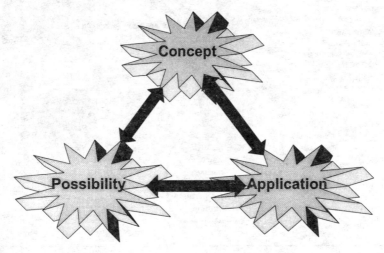

Concept

The concept is the basic 'idea', the creative element. It may be a totally new concept (although this is in fact quite rare), or it may be the combination of existing elements, such as transferring an idea that works in one context into another, or using new media or materials to provide an existing product in an new way. The concept is the 'what-if' factor, the inspiration or new idea derived from imagination or from the thought that 'there must be a better way' of achieving a frustrating task. The concept introduces something different.

Application

The application is the market opportunity which is created, or which exists, for the concept. Fundamentally, there must be customers who will perceive the concept as adding value and who will aspire to own or use it. It needs to be an improvement on the current 'state of the art' and to deliver changes that customers will see as benefits, not simply novelty for its own sake. Capability in marketing is vital for finding and exploiting applications successfully, by relating the concept to real needs and aspirations: who will buy it, what are their needs?

Possibility

The possibility is the 'how-to' technology, in its widest sense, which enables the concept to become reality. The technology needs to be available and usable and, in this way, technology is both an enabler and a constraint to innovation. If available, it enables it to take place. If it is not available to the required level, successful innovation is not yet possible until technological progress is made.

Exercise

Take some time out to think creatively. Start by writing down one element – either a concept ('what-if'), a market need or a technology – then brainstorm. Come up with as many alternatives for the other two elements as you can, without discounting any.

So if you start with the concept, such as 'a better way of keeping teenagers' rooms tidy' (or whatever), list all the:

- possible market applications for the idea;
- possible technologies – ways in which it could be realised.

Then see if you can configure the elements to come up with new product ideas.

Direct Line

Peter Woods formed Direct Line as a subsidiary of the Royal Bank of Scotland in 1985. He noticed that in the US you could buy car insurance policies by telephone, without visiting a broker, and at low margins. This was made possible by expert computer systems that enabled call centre staff to issue standardised policies by asking a series of questions prompted by the computer system. Woods transferred the idea to the UK and pioneered 'insurance by phone', setting up a call centre and using peak television advertising with the trademark of a musical red phone on wheels. Direct Line transformed a complacent industry and aggressively took market share from traditional brokers. It then applied the same formula to other insurance and financial services such as banking and mortgages.

Concept: Insurance by phone.
Possibility: Call centre and expert system IT technology.
Application: Standardised insurance policy service at lower cost.

Successful innovations must have all of the above three elements fully developed and working in harmony. Unsuccessful innovations are always deficient or out of balance in at least one of the three elements. Any innovation can be understood and analysed in terms of its essential elements. Below are some examples.

Innovation	Concept	Application	Possibility	Result
Dyson vacuum cleaner.	Vacuum cleaner equally efficient at all stages in cleaning cycle.	Domestic user looking for more effective cleaning device and design-led approach.	Dual cyclone turbine process developed by Dyson.	Successful innovation changed market for vacuum cleaners.
Pyramid shaped tea bag.	Unusually shaped tea bag which offers enhanced flavour diffusion.	Differentiates Brooke Bond from other tea bags by novelty.	Enhanced tea bag manufacturing process.	Novelty product without clear value added.
Internet bookstore	Selling biggest selection of books at low costs via a website.	Enables book buyers to browse and buy from large catalogue at any time.	Web browser, search technology and dispatch services.	Pioneering innovation will succeed by attracting high usership.
Motorised skate-board	Electrically powered skateboard as personal, portable transportation.	Fashionable personal travel and leisure accessory.	Small electric traction motor and battery attached to skateboard.	Lacks clear application – a fad.

> ### Exercise
> For your opportunity, analyse:
>
> • What is the creative concept?
> • What is the technical possibility needed to provide it?
> • What are all the different technologies that could achieve this?
> • What are all the possible market applications you can think of?
> • Are all three elements equally well developed?
> • Does the synergy between them create an innovation which is:
>   • clearly differentiated from existing suppliers?
>   • attractive to the customer?
>   • technically feasible?

2. RECOGNISING MARKET AND PRODUCT OPPORTUNITIES

Ansoff[1] developed the product/market matrix model, which has become a generic strategic concept. It expresses four basic options for product and market development and in the modified form shown here can be used to recognise and assess opportunities.

Figure 3.5: The product/market matrix (Ansoff)

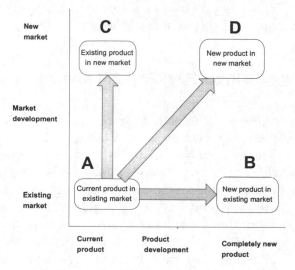

The rationale for each of the four options is summarised below. They show the implications of entering a market using that option.

Option A: Introducing a Current Product into an Existing Market

This introduces 'more of the same', copying what someone else is doing, with no product differentiation and without opening new markets for the product. It is likely to lead to head to head competition with existing operators and competition with them to gain market share. The new entrant will have disadvantages in their lack of existing customer relationships and market presence. There will be a strong risk of competitor reaction through predatory pricing, which may force them out of the market.

However, there are situations where Option A can work, where one or more of the following factors apply.

- Where competitors are underperforming, complacent businesses: the 'big bad wolf theory', which Virgin have used to target dominant businesses which can be challenged.

---

1. Ansoff, *Exploring Corporate Strategy* (1963) and as modified in Vyakarnam & Leppard, *A Marketing Action Plan for the Growing Business* (1995).

- Where scope exist for lower prices through process efficiencies or lower operating costs.
- Where is a growing market with room for more suppliers.

It is rather dangerous to enter an existing market with an undifferentiated product even in these situations since the scope for growth is likely to be limited. In the UK, the market for personal Internet access had been dominated by paid-for service providers until Dixons, and then Tesco, introduced a free service, and succeeded in gaining a large market share over the existing providers. They initially targeted their own retail customer base, and differentiated the service by making it free to the user.

Option B: Introducing a New Product into an Existing Market

This involves creating a completely new product or service and introducing it into an existing marketplace. A key capability for exploiting this option successfully is to be able to differentiate through the use of innovation. A transitional option between A and B is to adapt or modify where existing product offerings so as to differentiate them from existing products. Option B tends to create higher value-added products which are either complementary to, or which may replace, a current product. It requires there to be an existing market which can be entered and preferably one where customer demand is growing, such as where there is greater customer spending power (potential value) than is being taken up by existing products.

Option B depends on there being an underexploited market in which customers are prepared to buy a new, higher value product, but existing operators have not yet recognised this. It will tend to be stimulated by emerging technologies and the resulting possibilities these create, hence it is attractive to entrepreneurs on the leading-edge of technological change. The opportunity is to use innovation to develop new product/service combinations which customers are prepared to buy, thus adding value. This could be by adding knowledge-based services, such as consultancy and training, to a packaged product, for example computer software. Or a new delivery system, such as the Internet, may be used to access an existing market. To be successful, it is essential not only to be innovative but to have a fundamental understanding of customer needs, to understand 'everything they could want' as well as the decision making criteria they use in buying, and to offer high levels of customer relationship management to build the long-term value of customer spending.

- What do customers want or aspire to have?

- What don't they know about now but may need in future?
- How to persuade them to buy?

The disadvantages of Option B tend to be the investment, time and risk associated with developing and launching a new product, together with the likely competitor response, which may be to copy the innovation. A successful example of Option B was the launch in 1998 of the 'Egg' phone-based personal savings account by Prudential Insurance. Prudential had not previously offered a direct savings account, and entered the market with an innovatively packaged product paying above-market interest rates which was successful in winning large numbers of investors.

Option C: Introducing an Existing Product to a New Market

Option C suggests that the product is underexploited and there are potential new markets into which it can be introduced successfully. The transitional stage between A and C is to extend existing markets, for example by selling to competitors of current customers, further up the supply chain, through different distributors. Option C involves asking certain questions: What is the sales universe for this product? What are all the potential markets for it? Which are the best ones to enter? (see Chapter 6). Essentially it involves market-switching: creating and growing a new market for the product. It is, therefore, highly dependent for success on having the capabilities to understand the market, to launch, promote and distribute the product, to sell effectively and to build strong customer relationships which enhance loyalty and word of mouth marketing.

For Option C to be successful, the product itself needs to be current, although product life cycles can be extended by successive promotion into new markets. Each new market is likely to be culturally different and understanding cultural norms and customer buying processes is vital. It might involve, for example, a specialist building company, which has built up a domestic sector business, entering the public sector market. The likely response from operators in the new markets entered may be to attempt to source and supply similar products themselves and to use their stronger market presence to destroy the new entrant. The threat of this may be reduced by some form of joint venture or sales agreement with an existing, non-competing operator in the market and by using their distribution and sales capability to enter the market successfully with both lower risk and investment. An example of Option C is to import exotic Mexican and Thai ethnic foods. into the UK and supply restaurants and take away outlets.

Option D: Launching a New Product into a New Market

This involves finding and creating a new market and launching a new product into it. It requires the greatest capability in terms of both product innovation and marketing and sales, effectively doubling the risk. Customer segmentation, identifying the characteristics of groups of potential customers, is essential to understand and relate the product promotion to the customers' aspirations. Learning the essential characteristics and critical success factors of the product to introduce it successfully, are equally essential. The first new entrant with a new product carries the highest risk of failure. They require deep resources to support the product and market development, and they must be prepared to lose all of them if the demand cannot be created or the product is ineffective.

There are three likely scenarios for new entrants into a new market.

1. **Trailblazer**: the first entrant pioneers the product, creates an initial demand, e.g. for a limited product at a high price. They may make expensive mistakes and learn the hard way, but do not have the resources to exploit the market fully when the results start to indicate to other operators that there is a potential market which they start to enter and, by having superior resources, exploit more effectively. Trailblazer sells out or withdraws. For example, the magnetic levitating train, pioneered then abandoned in the UK, later adopted in Germany and Japan.

2. **Dominator**: the first entrant innovates successfully, introduces the product effectively and creates a market. It has enough resources to support the product while initial results are unpromising and setbacks are experienced and resolved. This initial period enables the pioneer to establish a position of technical and market strength whilst others are considering or preparing to enter the market. Subsequent entrants are unable to challenge successfully this dominant leadership. For example, Murdoch with Sky satellite television.

3. **Failure**: the pioneer fails either to introduce a workable product effectively or to create a market. It encounters problems and runs out of resources to overcome them. Withdraws having lost total investment. For example, the Sinclair C5 electric car.

Exercise
Which of the four options most closely describes the opportunity you have identified?

> - Option A: current product in existing market.
> - Option B: new product in existing market.
> - Option C: existing product in new market.
> - Option D: new product in new market.
>
> What are the advantages and disadvantages of this market position for the potential venture?

3. ASSESSING THE POTENTIAL OF OPPORTUNITIES

Identifying an opportunity leads naturally into assessing its potential. This requires that many factors must be considered and evaluated. Failure to identify and judge the factors correctly is likely to result in a 'wrong' decision being made and a greater likelihood of a venture being launched when the prospects for success are poor. Alternatively, a promising opportunity may be missed. These decisions are made in a dynamic rather than static environment, where key factors can be changed by the behaviour of both the entrepreneur (for example, by introducing a new product to a market), and by external factors, such as the economy, competitor or customer behaviour.

Before investing time, effort and money in a venture, the entrepreneur needs to assess the potential of the venture as an investment proposition. This cannot be overemphasised; it is a business decision, requiring dispassionate and objective analysis. The return on investment must be considerably greater than a 'safe' investment, such as buying government bonds. The risks have to be factored in, and either minimised or accepted. It is easy to get carried away with enthusiasm for the potential of an opportunity and to neglect the risks representing the 'downside', only to discover these later. On the other hand, over-analysis can lead to very slow decision making or even a failure to act at all. Speed of decision making and of acting is vital for entrepreneurial success; timing is the 'secret weapon' of the entrepreneur. Being right and doing it right, at the right moment, are all equally important. In some situations, it may be better to act and to learn quickly from what happens, and then to modify the strategy, than to fail to act at all.

There are many questions that can be asked in assessing a potential venture. This section introduces an initial set of questions, which can be used in assessing a venture, following which an analytical model is developed.

Assessing the venture

Customer information

- Who are the target, ideal customers?
- How can they be segmented?

- What is known about these customers?
- What do they want or need?
- Why do they want or need it?
- How are their needs met currently?
- How do they decide what, how and from whom to buy?

Market information

- What is the size of the market, how many customers are there?
- What is the total value of market? Is it growing, static or declining?
- What is the lifetime of the market?
- Is the product unique, desirable, essential or a discretionary commodity?
- What are the key factors that drive demand and price in the market?
- What is the strength of competition in the market?
- Which are the dominant firms that supply and control the market?
- What are their strengths and weaknesses?
- How will competitors respond to a new entrant to the market?

The venture

Customers

- How is the new venture differentiated, representing an improvement over the existing situation?
- What advantages does this advantage offer customers?
- How will customers be persuaded of this?
- What is the added value to customers? How much is it worth to them?
- How will the product be priced?
- What percentage of the market volume and spend will the business aim to secure each year?
- What selling and distribution channels will be used to reach all the target customer segments?
- What are the costs of gaining and selling to a new customer?
- What are the costs of producing and delivering the product to a customer?
- Is the buying customer relationship (loyalty) or transaction (one-off) based?
- What factors will affect customer retention, repeat and added-value purchases?
- What are the costs of servicing and retaining customers?

Investment

- How much investment is needed to develop and launch the venture?

- How much time is there to develop and launch? What is the window of opportunity?
- How fast can others replicate it? Who else is already working on it?
- What are the key factors that will drive the success of the venture?
- At what point in time and sales volume will the business breakeven and make a profit?
- When will the cash flow move from negative to positive?
- What return on investment will the business make? Over what timescale?
- What growth in the value of the business? Over what timescale, is expected?

The list of questions shown above is not comprehensive, but it does begin to show the range of information required to assess the potential of a venture and to present it to potential investors in terms which will have meaning for them. In other words, it is the starting point for researching and preparing a business plan, which is continued later in this chapter and in Chapter 8.

Exercise
- Starting with the list above, draw up your own list of the questions you would need to answer in assessing the potential of your proposed venture.
- You are not likely to be able to answer many of these at this stage; they will require further research.
- How will you find the information required to answer these questions?

Five Key Dimensions of Venture Potential

Although, as the above list of questions shows, there are many factors which could apply, there are five key dimensions in which the potential for ventures aiming to exploit opportunities can be assessed. By using these, ventures can be weighed up as an investment propositions and a decision reached as to their attractiveness – initially by the entrepreneur, and subsequently by other investors. These five dimensions, which form the basis of a mapping model for decision making, are described below. A questionnaire based on the five dimensions is given in Appendix 3.

Figure 3.6: The five dimensions of opportunity

- **Investment:**   from none to high.
- **Risk:**   from certainty to unpredictability.
- **Return:**   from none to high.
- **Degree of change caused:**   from none to great.
- **Time:**   from now into the future.

Investment: from none to high

Whatever the opportunity, some form of investment will be required to realise it. The nature of the investment may be a combination of the following.

- Financial: capital belonging to the entrepreneur, venture capital from an investor, equity or loan finance.
- Non-financial resources, such as productive capacity, time and capability (representing an opportunity cost since the resources could be used alternatively for a different reward).
- An intangible factor, such as knowledge, information, expertise.
- Reputation and credibility.

The power of branding shows that such intangible factors can have considerable value: for example, an accredited Microsoft Office-compatible software product will have greater market attraction than one without it.

The size of the investment, as well as its nature, is significant: how much is required, over what period? What proportion of the entrepreneur's own resources does this represent, or are additional resources required? If so, who will contribute them, and on what terms? Finally, what does the investment actually buy? Is it tangible assets that have a disposal value or simply an opportunity? This leads on to the concept of risk.

Risk: from certainty to unpredictability

The entrepreneur needs to be able to evaluate the degree of risk involved. Risk is caused by uncertainty: where there is complete certainty (if such a thing exists) there is an absence of risk, conversely, complete unpredictability of outcome produces a very high degree of risk. In a financial market, a UK or US government bond has a guaranteed rate of return and offers much greater certainty and hence less risk than, for example, a 'junk bond' or newly floated biotechnology stock where the outcome is highly uncertain and there is high risk. The stereotype of the entrepreneur is often as a risk-taker, even a reckless gambler prepared to stake all on madcap schemes. This has little bearing in fact; successful entrepreneurs will seek to minimise and avoid risk as far as possible, preferring other investors to carry the financial exposure. However, the entrepreneur frequently operates in conditions of change and uncertainty which do give rise to unpredictable outcomes. Also, where the venture introduces change into the marketplace, it is also introducing new risk factors because the outcome is to some extent unpredictable.

Identifying the Risk Factors

The variable factors, which cause risk, need to be identified. They may include:

- lack of information about market factors and likely demand;
- fluctuations in macro-economic factors such as market stability, currency exchange and interest rates;
- technological uncertainty;
- competitor activity and response;
- customer, supplier and distributor dependability: the risk of non-delivery, e.g. of orders, supplies, payment.

Every potential risk to the venture should be identified, including such basics as the loss of key personnel to the venture. The risks can then be divided into:

- **controllable risks**: which the entrepreneur can act to reduce or eliminate. Examples would be lack of market or product information where focused research can take place, and customer, supplier or distributor dependability where again research, credit rating and negotiation can reduce risk;
- **uncontrollable risks**: these are a function of factors in the economic environment together with the plain unpredictable. For each of these entrepreneur needs to establish:
  - How serious is the risk – could it sink the business?
  - How likely is it?
  - What are likely to be the earliest warning signs of the event?
  - What contingency plans can be drawn up to respond to the event?
  - How can the effects of the risk on the business be minimised or insured against?

In these ways the risks to the venture can be established and either prevented or their effects can be assessed and plans to deal with them made. However risk can never be eliminated or even predicted entirely.

Return: from none to high

The return on the investment, or reward, may vary from none (a total loss of the investment) to high (which may be a return of several hundred per cent.) An assessment of the acceptability of the return is likely to take into account the following factors:

- **the amount invested**: it may be acceptable to lose a small investment completely. Millions of people do this every time they buy a lottery ticket;
- **return in relation to risk**: the higher the risk, the higher the return expected will be;
- **over what timescale the return will come**: risk increases over time;
- **form of the return**: for example, as capital growth of the investment or as a flow of income. An asset such as property or equity in a company might be expected to show both capital growth through a rise in its value together with an income flow from dividends or rentals.

The matrix below shows the basic dimensions of risk and reward.

In this model, clearly position 1, offering a high return at low risk, is the optimum. Positions 2 and 3 are both less attractive, 2 offering low risk but at low return, and 3 offering high return but at high risk. Position 4 is clearly to be avoided since the prospects are high risk and low return. However, such a two-dimensional model is inevitably an oversimplification, since other factors always have an effect.

Degree of change: from none to great

Exploiting an opportunity both creates change and is, itself, affected by other changes in the market environment. Introducing a completely new concept as a product, such as the first Psion handheld personal organiser or Direct Line insurance, introduced fundamental changes into the market. An enhancement to a current product is a moderate, incremental change and a replication of something that already exists represents little or no change.

It is necessary to think through what changes the venture may lead to. Is the venture driving in and leading change through its actions, or is it passive, causing little change but rather affected by external change? Strategic innovators can make the competition – temporarily – powerless and create new markets. A process innovation, which enables a new business to offer lower prices than existing suppliers, will attract existing, and probably new, customers, thus changing customer expectations and behaviour. The introduction of budget air carriers, such as EasyJet, has expanded the air travel market, polarising customer expectations between low-cost, no-frills service and high-cost standard service. An innovation may make previous standard products obsolete. The impact of such changes can be felt throughout the supply chain, affecting suppliers, re-sellers, customers, sources of finance, as well as competitors. A new venture offering something different also invites retaliation from competitors, as EasyJet found when British Airways retaliated with its own 'Go' budget airline.

The effects of introducing such change into the market are to some extent unpredictable; they increase risk rather than reducing it. Also any business is also subject to external changes (such as macro-economic factors and market trends influencing customer behaviour, supply and demand changes leading to price fluctuations, technological advance, and changes in legislation, regulation, and so on) which can be assessed under the heading 'risk'.

Time: from now into the future

The timescale for the venture needs to be assessed. Achieving the right timing is often a critical factor in entrepreneurial decision making, and points to consider here include the following.

- Is the timing of entry leading 'the rest' of the market, which may give an advantage but also require greater investment? Is it entering the market at the same time as competitors, or is it trailing others into a mature or declining market?
- What is the duration of the opportunity – from short-term to indefinite?
- What is the lead-time needed to prepare to enter the market?
- When will the investment achieve a return, and what is its life span?
- What is the best time to leave the market?

Return and timescale

The return on the investment together with the expected timescale needs to be established as realistically as possible. 'Best case', 'most likely' and 'worst case' scenarios can be built into these forecasts which project:

- the investment required over time;
- the sales revenue to be generated as a cash stream;
- the gross profit margin on sales;
- the breakeven point;
- the net profit margin;
- return on capital employed;
- growth in the asset value of the investment.

The time period is highly significant. It may be that, in establishing a new venture, a loss is made in the first year (requiring further working capital), breakeven in year 2, and profit from year 3. The longer the investment period, the higher the rate of return needs to be. The nature of the gain to the investor needs to be clear, in terms of returns from trading profits and growth in the value of the investment, which can be realised through sale of the asset at some point. Most businesses take longer to launch and consume more start-up capital than projected, a phenomenon known as 'death valley curve'; they run out of cash before they can achieve breakeven. Computer spreadsheets make forecasting straightforward, as long as accurate and realistic data can be obtained. An example is shown for 'the pizza shop' a little later in this chapter.

The five dimensions described can be used in evaluating the prospects for successfully exploiting an opportunity and, therefore, in deciding whether to venture. The decision making process is a complex one. It is likely that almost every entrepreneur would weigh up a venture in a different way. It is clear that the process is not one that can be simplified as a bivariate '2x2' matrix such as 'risk related to return' alone. It is a multivariate process. By taking the five dimensions described above as the variables, a pentagon-shaped multivariate model for assessing opportunities can be constructed using these factors, and is shown below.

Figure 3.7: The pentagon model of opportunity assessment

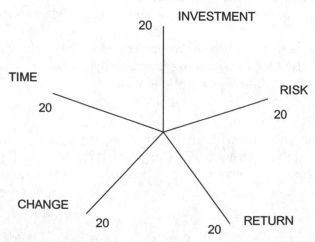

Using the questionnaire in Appendix 3, a profile can be drawn on the pentagon model. Each dimension can be given a scale from zero to twenty. Zero is 'none' and twenty is 'high'. Any given opportunity can then be given a series of values along the score. These, in themselves, will involve a series of objective, factual and subjective, interpretative judgements being made, involving available information, past experience, projective judgement, and so on. They may be relatively unscientific, but they do form judgements that would be made, often on the basis of 'gut feeling', intuition or experience, by an entrepreneur. The scores along each dimension then represent a distinctive pattern. Two examples are given below.

1. Pizza take-away: a small business

The opportunity is to open a take-away pizza outlet in a town High Street, which currently has no existing fast food pizza outlet. There is busy passing trade so prospects look good. The capital investment to refit the shop is £30,000 and there is a 5-year lease with a rental of £12,000 p.a. The investment can be financed by the promoter together with access to bank lending for working capital. It is expected to show a first year net profit of £8,000, providing a return on capital of 24 per cent, but there is little scope for growth in long-term value as future trading is dependent on renewal of the lease.

Year	1	2	3	4	5
Investment required	30,000				
Sales revenue	80,000	90,000	100,000	110,000	120,000
Fixed expenses	40,000	42,000	44,000	46,000	48,000
Variable costs	32,000	36,000	40,000	44,000	48,000
Total costs	72,000	78,000	84,000	90,000	96,000
Gross margin	60%	60%	60%	60%	60%
Breakeven sales	66,000	70,000	73,333	76,666	80,000
Net margin	10%	13%	16%	18%	20%
Profit/(loss)	8000	12,000	16,000	20,000	24,000
Net return on investment	26%	40%	53%	66%	80%
Value of assets	30,000	22,500	15,000	7,500	0

- Investment — Moderate — 8
- Risk — Low — 5
- Return — Medium-high — 15
- Degree of change — Low — 5
- Time — Short/medium-term — 8

Figure 3.8: Pentagon profile for the pizza take-away

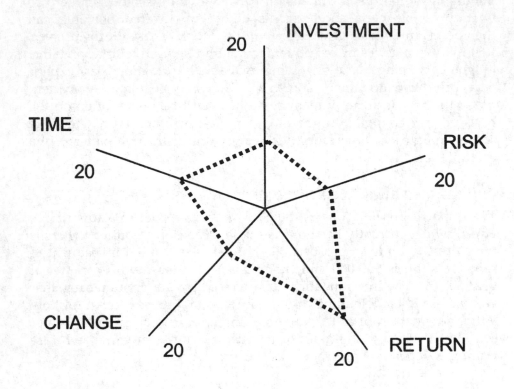

2. The digital radio

An inventor noticed that not only were electronics companies very slow to bring a portable digital radio receiver to market, the receiver could also be allied with Internet technology to allow users to send and receive e-mail messages and undertake Internet searches. He developed a prototype and prepared an investment proposal which claimed the following.

- **Investment required**: £5 million (high)   score 20
- **Return**: profit of £4 million by year 3.
  plus growing value of intellectual property
  and design rights   score 16
- **Risk of imitation or product failure**: high   score 18
- **Change**: major   score 17
- **Time**: medium-term return   score 14

Figure 3.9: Pentagon profile for the digital radio business

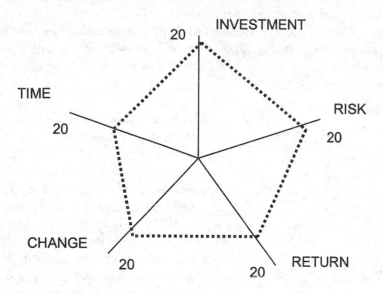

In comparing the profiles of the two opportunities, it can be seen that they differ in almost all respects except the return. The pizza take-away represents a relatively low-risk, low-investment venture with an excellent cash return but no longer term prospect of growth. The digital radio is higher on the scales of risk, investment, change and timescale. The area enclosed by the lines is greater for the radio than the pizza take-away.

Opportunities, which have characteristics of greater risk, higher reward, bigger investment, larger scale change, and medium/longer timescales, can be described as being more 'aggressive' in the venture strategies that would be required to launch them, and will have a large profile when drawn on the pentagon. Those with lower degrees of investment, risk, reward, change and short/medium timescales can be described as more 'defensive', with a tightly grouped profile on the pentagon. There are also many combinations that have elements of both.

The pizza take-away has a defensive profile, scoring low in all aspects except return, and would not require sophisticated entrepreneurial strategy or skills to be successful. The radio has a larger profile, indicating a more aggressive strategy, which would require much more advanced capability to be successful. Each opportunity, therefore, will have its own profile, representing a view at that moment of its potential. If a venture is launched to exploit the opportunity, each of the variables has its own dynamic and may shift in either direction at any stage in the life of the venture.

Some profiles will be more attractive to certain types of investors and entrepreneurs than others; a few should be avoided altogether. Interpreting the profiles is subjective, but it enables the variables to be assessed and compared. Some investors would alter the dimensions, for example a venture capitalist might replace the 'change' dimension with 'capability of the entrepreneurial team'. Also, in making investment decisions, it is always sensible to look at the alternatives, including leaving your money in safe government bonds. Any such alternatives can be mapped using this model. Three examples of different profiles are shown below as examples.

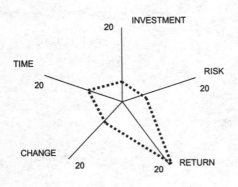

The ideal 'safe return'

This combines low investment with low risk, little change and high return within a short timescale. Bankers and fund managers love these types of investments, unfortunately there are few that actually deliver the results they indicate. It indicates a short-term opportunistic strategy, based on trading or arbitrage. Is it too good to be true, with the return overstated and risk understated?

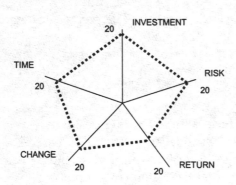

To be avoided

This scores high on everything except results. There is high investment, uncertainty, change and it is over a long-term – ambitious overall but with a mediocre payback. Leave such projects to the public sector. Projects such as the Channel Tunnel, UK atomic energy and reprocessing industries have profiles like this. They demand patient investors.

Strategic opportunity

This profile shows an entrepreneurial opportunity. The investment is fairly high, requiring external input, over a fairly long timescale and with moderate risk and change. The return is acceptably high. If the people running the venture have the managerial calibre required, it may well be a high-returning and medium-term investment.

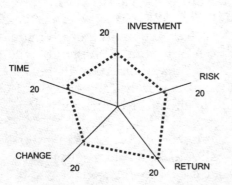

Exercise

Use the opportunity assessment questionnaire in Appendix 3 to assess your opportunity.

- Answer the questions on each dimension.
- Total the scores for each dimension and plot these onto the pentagon.
- Join the plotting points to show its profile.
- What does the profile suggest about the potential for exploiting this opportunity? Is it defensive or aggressive? Is it an attractive investment, and to what type of investor? Would you invest your money in it?

---

4. EXPLOITING OPPORTUNITIES

Synergising the Opportunity, Capability and Resources, Designing the Organisation

Having identified and evaluated an opportunity and decided to exploit it, the question is: How to do it? Essential for successful entrepreneurship is unlocking, bringing together, and harnessing the different elements that, when combined, create a successful venture. Also the entrepreneur must provide the leadership which is vital to achieve this. Three key elements are the opportunity, the resources and the organisation as shown below.

Figure 3.10: The entrepreneurial process[2]

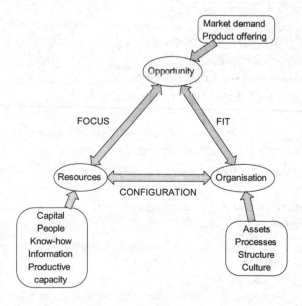

---

2. Adapted from Wickham, *Strategic Entrepreneurship* (1997).

The opportunity, as described earlier in this chapter, is, fundamentally, a market demand which is met through some form of product offering. To exploit this opportunity, resources of various kinds are required – finance, expertise, information, people, operational capacity, and supply of inputs, which are processed to provide the product offering. To achieve this successfully, even the most basic enterprise needs organisation – of physical assets (such as equipment or premises), processes (to ensure customer demand is met profitably), a structure (to ensure people know what they have to do) and a culture or set of values (which, at the most basic survival level, might simply be the entrepreneur's drive to make sales and bring in cash quickly).

It is clear from this concept, that any venture needs to be *designed*; no two enterprises will ever be identical since each is designed uniquely to exploit an identified market opportunity, by configuring and organising its resources in a way that is clearly focused and creates a fit between the organisation and the opportunity. All the new ventures, which will be described in Chapter 5, were designed in some way by their founders as the most effective way of meeting the market need. A successful enterprise rarely 'just happens'. With businesses, which aim to create new markets or to gain high levels of customers through being easy to buy from, carefully designing the business is an important factor in planning for its success. Effective design will differentiate the business from competitors, who grew organically to be the way they are, and result in process efficiency, cost advantage and customer-side virtues of being friendly, personal, and easy to do business with.

IKEA[3]

Visit an IKEA furniture warehouse. Every aspect of the business is carefully designed around certain key principles, which implement its strategy, shape its operations and maximise its financial performance. These principles include the following.

- International, Swedish-flavour design creates a globally acceptable product, giving huge supply-chain economies.
- High levels of customer information, low sales and service staff costs.
- Flatpack furniture design and assembly reduces storage and distribution costs, the customer takes it home and does all the work.
- Stores designed for efficient customer through flow and to boost impulse purchases.

Within the UK alone, IKEA came to dominate the self-assembly furniture market within ten years of opening its first store.

---

3. Porter, "What is Strategy" *Harvard Business Review* (November/December 1997).

Exercise

Take the venture you are developing in this chapter and start to design it as an enterprise. Use visual tools, such as mapping (see the planning model below), simple flow diagram and other techniques you may have found (such as rich pictures or activity system mapping) to develop your ideas. For example you could draw a flow diagram to follow 'a customer's journey' through the business, then add the other aspects of the business to this.

- What are the key processes in the business?
- How can these be organised most efficiently?
- How can the interface with the customer be organised to maximise buyer attractiveness?
- What resources are needed?

Figure 3.11: Venture planning

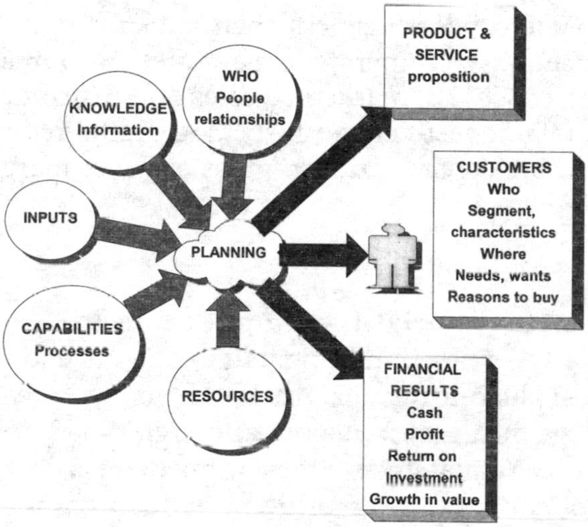

Planning the Venture

Designing the venture leads logically into planning the business. Knowing how the business will work, what the key processes are and how they will function is essential in order to develop a business plan. There are many books and guides on business planning, and again, this book does not aim to replicate them. However, planning is a vital stage in the process of creating a new venture, for the following reasons.

- It develops a clear case for the business, its rationale and potential for success, forcing the entrepreneur to justify their assumptions.
- It enables investors and lenders to form a view about the business' prospects and decide whether to support it.

- It becomes a management tool, giving a sense of purpose and projections against which results can be monitored and plans modified.

Effective business plans are generally the product of a good deal of research as well as of thinking through different scenarios and arguments. Chapter 8 will explore developing a business plan for your venture as one outcome of reading this book. At that stage, the contents of a typical plan for a business with growth aims are listed. This is intended to help you to start thinking through and bringing together the components of your plan.

The growth business plan

- The vision for the business, its goals and targets.
- The opportunity for the business.
- The investment proposition: risk and return.
- Market research and analysis of the need.
- Competitor and industry structure analysis.
- Differentiation.
- People: who will run the business, their track records.
- How the business will operate: capabilities, resources, people and management, processes, marketing, sales and distribution.
- Financial: capital investment and working capital requirements, cash flow forecast, breakeven, pricing, gross and net margins, return on investment.

5. TRADING

The oldest entrepreneurial function, dating back to at least the Phoenician Empire, is that of trading, buying goods and re-selling them at a higher price. Historically, this has not depended greatly on innovation except for the means of transport, although this is now changing as a result of technology that gives almost immediate access to buying and selling prices of commodities worldwide. Much economic theory has been expended in explaining the trading process and the role of the entrepreneur. In its simplest terms, the trading dynamic can be expressed as the relationship between supply and demand: the cost at which goods are bought from suppliers and the market price.

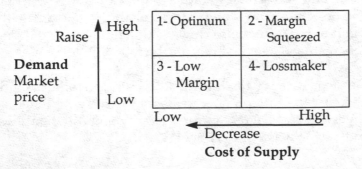

The old maxim of the trader is to 'buy cheap, sell dear'. Key factors in successful trading are the ability to:

- maximise profit margins;
- maximise cash revenue to finance buying;
- minimise liabilities, e.g. borrowing and unsold stocks;
- predict market trends through foresight and act ahead of the market;
- out-think and out-sell competitors;
- be first to the market to optimise premium pricing, be prepared to leave markets as competition erodes margins;
- make it easy and attractive for the customer to buy – availability, speed, convenience, reliability, recognised branding and service quality all add perceived value which enables the market price to be increased;
- change buying sources and enhance communication processes to maintain cost and speed advantages.

One form of trading is based on the theory of arbitrage, which seeks to exploit pricing disparities – which usually disappear through the arbitrageur's actions – in a marketplace. Arbitrage aims to sell items at a price higher than they may be purchased for in a marketplace, and is largely confined to financial markets.

Price Erosion of Premium Products

There is a trend for products that, initially, may be positioned in the market at a premium level, quickly to become 'commoditised' and to move to a price level which is set by competition in the market, through competitors using the economies of large-scale production to replicate the original product. An example of this is the Nike 'Airflow' trainer shoe. To the entrepreneur with a 'world-beating idea' this may be disheartening – but it is a normal process, which is being accelerated by technical advances and global production capacity of both products and services. There are four basic strategies that can be adopted to respond to this erosion. When launching a new product into the market, the follow-on strategy needs to be planned just as carefully as the launch.

- Possession of a sought-after brand name, intellectual property and design rights to defend the premium position.
- Continual innovation, improvement and value-addition to stay ahead of competitors.
- Selling or licensing the product rights to realise the asset value before commoditisation takes place and move onto something else.
- Using process innovation and cost reduction to compete on price.

Arguably, there is little that is really new in effective market-making and trading capabilities. Fundamentally, the same rules and principles apply now in financial and retail markets, for example, as have applied through history. They simply operate very much faster and are based on a vastly greater quantity of information and many more choices. Learning how markets work, and how to trade successfully in them, is achieved by immersion, by the experience of working in them, by failing and succeeding rather than by theoretical understanding. Therefore, for the entrepreneur, in-depth understanding of the market in which their business will operate is absolutely essential.

If you have worked in the industry and market in which your business will trade, it is vital to think through the market drivers and 'rules' and to analyse how they will affect your business, and any ways in which you can take advantage of them. If, on the other hand, you contemplate entering a market of which you do not have a thorough understanding or experience, beware. An essential step would be to spend time researching and, if possible, working in that market – even unpaid – to develop your understanding of how it works.

Exercise

What strategies would you adopt in the marketplace to achieve profitable trading for the opportunity you have identified?

REVIEW

Take a few minutes to reflect on the concepts and exercises you have used in this chapter to explore and develop the potential of a venture.

What thinking processes and decision making models you would use to:

- identify opportunities in markets for products?
- create opportunities through innovation?
- assess and decide on opportunities?
- design and plan a business?
- trade successfully?

CHAPTER 4

The Entrepreneurial Process: Connecting Personal and Business Goals

The aim of this chapter is to explore the interrelationships between the personal goals of the entrepreneur and the approaches they adopt in starting, growing and moving out of business ventures. It discusses the connection between the entrepreneur, as an individual, and the need to build some form of organisation in order to fulfil their goals. It introduces the concept of entrepreneurial strategy as a series of choices, and summarises the debate about models of business growth. Finally, it creates a framework for interpreting and understanding the individual experience of the entrepreneur. This framework is then used in the following three chapters to follow the experiences and learning processes from the entrepreneur's point of view.

THE ENTREPRENEURIAL CHALLENGE

There are many people whose business consists simply of selling their own services on a freelance or self-employed basis; they probably constitute the vast majority of 'small businesses' in the UK, and their numbers are likely to continue to grow as the economic structure changes. Self-employed people run an incredibly diverse range of businesses, everything from market trading to language teaching, childcare to secretarial services, window cleaning to management consultancy. But can all of these people be considered entrepreneurs?

Following the arguments set out in Chapter 1 ('What or who is an entrepreneur?'), the position taken in this book is quite clear: it is the intention, the drive and the possession of 'entrepreneurial spirit' that makes the difference, and the self-employed person is much more likely than the average population to be entrepreneurial given that they have already taken the big, brave step of running themselves as a business venture.

The question, which they must face, is whether they are content for the business to be simply 'themselves', selling their own personal value, or whether they have the drive, ambition and can develop the capabilities needed to grow the business beyond this. That is the entrepreneurial decision.

Staying small is a legitimate choice, which is made by the owners of many small businesses, be they retailers, builders, subcontractors or independent professionals. It may be right for them, for it limits the investment of time and money and possibly the downside risks of growth. It is their decision, and since these small businesses make a huge contribution to the economy as wealth producers, employers and taxpayers, then no one should criticise them for choosing to stay small; this book praises them for what they are already doing. They do not aim to grow substantially, rather to survive and stay in control. However, the decision not to grow may limit the life of the business, which is unlikely to survive indefinitely without growing, but it is the element of choice that matters: as Watson commented:

> *We must abandon the notion that an organisation is like an animal: hav-*
> *ing necessarily to grow up from infancy through childhood into mature*
> *adulthood. No animal has the choice to stay small, those running a firm*
> *do.*[1]

However, entrepreneurial behaviour is, fundamentally, about growing the business, and that implicitly means the business must become bigger than the person. It is possible to be in business and indeed to make sub-stantial amounts of money as a deal-maker or consultant and to have nothing more than a mobile phone, a laptop computer, an astute brain and lots of contacts. However, whilst personal wealth and value in that sense can be built up, the business is still surviving on a short-term hori-zon through the efforts of one person. There are human limits to how much, and for how long, one person can do it. To achieve more, to be able to grow a business venture which has a continuing and appreciating value of its own, an organisation must be created which will be bigger than the entrepreneur. That is the entrepreneurial challenge.

THE ORGANISATION AND THE ENTREPRENEUR

An organisation can be defined in many ways – as an economic unit creating wealth, a social construction of people working together, a legal entity, an information system, and so on. If we see the business venture as a way of fulfilling the entrepreneur's personal goals, then, in forming an organisation, an important step is being taken to fulfil those goals through that organisation, not just through the person. The busi-ness must have goals and a strategy to be successful, and they will be determined largely if not completely by the entrepreneur, but they are part of the business, not of the person who created it. However, it is (very often) still 'my business', and its nature will be formed and defined largely by the entrepreneur's learning up to that point.

There is, inevitably, a close and continuing interplay between the

---

1. Watson, "Entreprenurialship and Professional Management: A Fatal Distinction" *ISBJ* (1995) Vol. 13, No. 2, pp. 34-46.

objectives of the business as a venture and the personal goals of the entrepreneur. Their goals may be such things as self-realisation, the growth of personal wealth, or the founding of a continuing family business. At the time of starting a business, the business goals are instrumental to achieving and are shaped by the superordinate personal agenda: if the aim of a 50 year old executive is to generate a retirement fund he is likely to select a business venture, such as buying into an existing business, which is most likely to achieve this, and will adopt a strategy and ways of running the business which are instrumental in achieving this personal aim.

The strategy itself will reflect the entrepreneur's previous learning, values and motivations, and will be implemented using habits formed by lifelong experience in working towards personal goals and encountering success and failure. However, although the business strategy is formed by the entrepreneur, and often influenced by others, the business and the entrepreneur constitute two separate entities. This is essential in understanding the entrepreneurial experience, since, although there is a close identification (even at times a fusion) between entrepreneur and business, this is not a permanent state, rather a phase in the entrepreneurial process.

Every business is given shape by a unique combination of the aspirations and capabilities of the founder(s), by the opportunities it aims to exploit, and by what is learned from the events and experiences that shape its development. If several people are involved in creating the business, for example as a team-based start-up, it will reflect their shared and differing aspirations and capabilities. The business is launched, tested in the marketplace and it may then fail, survive or thrive over time. These dynamic forces of goals, learning and capabilities will have formative influence on the growth strategy of an entrepreneurial business, as shown in the diagram below.

Figure 4.1: Influences on growth strategy

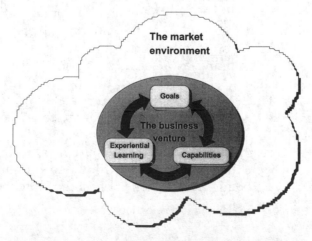

DEVELOPING A STRATEGY FOR GROWTH

Operating within the chosen market environment, there are three key personal forces which tend to guide the development of a strategy for the business by the entrepreneur. The first is the set of personal goals which they aim to achieve, reinforced by their motivational drivers. The second is the set of capabilities – skills and knowledge – which they have evolved and can apply. The third is the cognitive ability to learn by experience from the environment, and to form judgements about whether their goals are attainable or need to be modified, and how their capabilities can be used to achieve the goals. Through experiential learning, an understanding of how the market operates is developed, together with an appreciation of the impact (or lack of it) of their own actions in the market. The learning process enables theories to be developed, through which the norms, rules and trends in the market can be understood. Based on these theories, choices are made – consciously or unconsciously, rationally or intuitively – about the way the enterprise will be run, and what it must do to be successful.

This may be achieved, initially at least, through working as an individual, with sole responsibility for setting the strategy. But as soon as other people are involved in the organisation – whether they be as partners, employees, even freelance associates – strategy-making becomes at least in part a social process. For every person connected with the business has their own personal goals, capabilities and learning, which will govern their interaction with the business. The entrepreneur may believe that 'he is in control' and that all everyone else has to do is 'what they are told, on a need-to-know basis', or may see themselves as the dynamic 'powerhouse' of the business, setting the direction and energising everyone to achieve it; these are common self-perceptions. However the strategy is only enacted and accomplished through the efforts of everyone involved. So if the entrepreneur adopts a highly directive, dominant approach to managing others, this may lead to others showing compliance, not commitment and, ultimately, to an oppressive 'rule by fear' which seriously damages the organisation's health and ability to grow. It can work – as the late and largely unlamented Robert Maxwell found – but surely there is a better way?

If we see strategy-making as a social process, in which the goals, capabilities and learning of everyone can be engaged, a different scenario can be constructed. If the entrepreneur is able to act as leader, communicating the vision and creating the energy to achieve it, whilst drawing others in to contribute their ideas and insights, experience and motivation, a strategy can be developed which includes everyone involved and which they are far more likely to be committed to achieve. In this way, being entrepreneurial becomes infectious, part of the culture of the business.

Emma

Emma, a graduate in fashion and clothing design, specialised in knitwear design and gained commercial experience early in her career working for large businesses in the industry. After a few years she realised that she wanted to establish her own design studio, and went freelance. Highly talented and with a portfolio of innovative colour and fabric concepts, she nevertheless found 'it was hard to open doors' with corporate buyers in the UK market. She persevered, and after a difficult first year, found that buyers in North America 'were much more open to me, prepared to make judgements on the quality of the design' and the business started to take off.

Emma's intention had never been to work as a solo freelance designer, but to create a studio 'as a design source for our industry' and to involve other talented designers who together would produce a constant stream of innovative, commercially successful designs. During three years of growth, she drew together a team of designers who researched and created designs, exhibited internationally, and gained over 100 clients, including many famous fashion designers. The studio had an individual style, and the vision had become 'to create a studio with a vibrancy where we enjoy working towards the common goal'.

But four years after forming the business, she realised that in managing it she was 'in constant fire fighting mode, running after problems in all directions, trying to take all the responsibility. Everybody has been working as hard and as fast as they can, with coherence over design direction, yet lacking enough time to execute ideas fully, therefore not maximising our full market potential'. Something had to change before Emma became totally frazzled or a serious problem, which they were too busy to anticipate, hit them and put the business at risk. She joined a business growth programme for owner-managers, which gave her the thinking time and support to develop a business plan for the first time, to reflect on where the business was positioned, and to develop a stronger internal structure for the business.

Like many young professionals, her training and ability had made her very accomplished in her specialist field – but she had never been shown how to run a business, and had just picked it up, by trial as well as by some rather expensive errors. But now she understood the value of setting goals for the business, of planning how to achieve them with her colleagues, of building the team, and of having defined responsibilities, routines and controls to ensure the business could run smoothly – and without her constant involvement.

STRATEGY AS A SERIES OF CHOICES

Entrepreneurial strategy is formed of a series of decisions, of choices between alternatives. Strategy is about both what the goals are, as well as how to attain them. People with an entrepreneurial outlook, will tend to recognise situations as offering opportunities, whilst the opposite stance is to perceive every situation in terms of threats, boundaries, constraints and difficulties it presents. The choices that are available can be represented as a decision-tree or as a route map, a journey from where you are to wherever you want to go. There is rarely if ever a true absence of choice, it is more that we may fail to use imagination to recognise the choices which do indeed exist – there is always 'another way' of reaching our destination. Lateral thinking produces alternatives and offers ways round problems.

Reactive and Proactive Disposition

A factor in exercising choice is the disposition towards proactivity or reactivity. The entrepreneurial outlook is predisposed towards proactivity – preferring to act, to be doing something that makes a difference and creates a result. It carries the assumption that problems and obstacles can be overcome, that success can be achieved, that growth and profitability can be achieved and maximised. It seeks to steer, to be in control. External forces and their effects are understood, and strategies formed and enacted to gain from them or to overcome them. In terms of learning style, it is highly activist.

The reactive disposition accepts a position of lesser power to take control and to make a difference. Its assumption is ultimately fatalistic: 'what will be, will be'. It accepts that growth happens or does not happen, and there is only so much that you can do about it. It accepts that 'you can't buck the market'. It argues that sometimes – quite a lot of the time – the best course of action is to see what others do and go along with them since that is the easiest thing to do. Rather than seizing the initiative and creating change, it is about making choices and taking decisions only when they are inescapable.

The entrepreneurial approach is normally firmly proactive in style. However, there will be situations where a reactive mode is tactically more advisable. When trading in a volatile commodity market, for example, it can be better to 'wait and see' and to take a defensive position to minimise losses and decide when to re-enter the market.

So entrepreneurial strategy is fundamentally about choice. Analysis has its place, but what counts is what you do, how you do it, and how successful the result turns out to be. Entrepreneurs cannot often afford the luxury of 'waiting and seeing'; it is necessary to know what to do, to decide and to act. There are always multiple choices available, and they change constantly, therefore, it is vital to understand what they are. This may require creative thinking, especially if it appears there is only one possible course of action. It is essential at times, such as, for example, when the business has completely run out of cash, to break out of the trap labelled 'there is no alternative' which leads to giving up. There are always alternatives. By being clear about all the available choices and making them explicit, the best one can be selected. Sometimes it will be necessary to identify a hard choice and to implement it ruthlessly, knowing it to be hard and perhaps unpopular but nevertheless the correct choice for the business. For the entrepreneur, thinking and planning strategically is not a 'once a year' luxury, but an everyday necessity.

The Choice Model of Entrepreneurial Strategy

This is an example of a choice map. It shows the choices faced initially in starting a business venture.

1. Goals: what to achieve
- What are the entrepreneur's longer term goals?

2. Plan: how to achieve them
- How to achieve the goals?
- Choice of business form:
  - starting a business;
  - acquiring a business;
  - working in an existing business;
  - by other means.
- How the venture will be organised to match the demand?
- Who to involve – as investors, partners, suppliers, co-workers – choice of people?
- How to assess the success of the venture – choice of success criteria?
- Where to operate from – choice of location?
- When – choice of timing of market entry, and life span of the venture?

3. Outcome: what's the value?

- What is the value to be released?
- Why? What is the rationale?
- What is the proposition offered to the customer?
- What is the benefit or added value?
- How is this differentiated from existing operators?
- What are the available opportunities, and how to select the optimum?
- What to do – choice of the product or service to be offered?
- Who is it for? What is the marketplace, choice of the customer?

4. What are the implications?

Opportunity appraisal. What is the:

- Risk?
- Investment?
- Return?
- Timing?
- Change?

Exercise

- What are the key decisions you have to make regarding your business venture?

- Draw a decision map of the decisions and choices you can make to help you develop your strategy.

MODELLING BUSINESS GROWTH

The conventional wisdom is that businesses grow over time, and the life of a business is classically portrayed as a linear process of growth. However, this is a contentious topic since Storey[2] attests that only a small minority of businesses are capable of significant, sustained growth. Most models of business growth are linear, predicting a series of stages which a growing business is expected to encounter. First illustrated by Greiner,[3] and refined by others, the linear growth model takes the form shown below.

---

2. Storey, *Understanding the Small Business Sector* (1994).
3. Greiner, "Evolution and Revolution as Organisations Grow" *Harvard Business Review* (1972).

Figure 4.2: The linear growth model

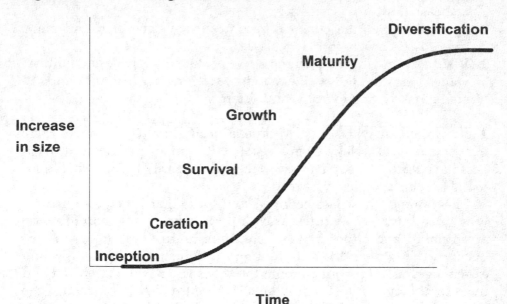

The Linear Growth Model

Linear growth models have a logical appeal, but even if we accept the simplification of measuring growth only along the two variables of increase in size (normally sales turnover) over time, they have serious limitations. Firstly, every business is unique and may not encounter the predicted stages. By simplifying the growth process, and suggesting it is preordained, linear models inevitably fail to convey the unique experiences, the choices and the learning process which are implicit in the launch, growth and life of a venture. Also, they do not reflect the economic factors of business cycles and market volatility. Many enterprises fail to survive their first three years and fail quickly. A few grow at high rates then, like firework rockets, explode spectacularly. Some grow quickly early in their lives until they reach a plateau where they stabilise, either to continue growing at a slower rate or to decline. Quite a lot of businesses experience periods of rapid growth linked to cyclical economic upturns followed by shrinkage in recessions. In summary, it is over-simplifying to say that there is a predictive, uniform model of growth.

An alternative to the linear growth model is the concept of 'glass ceilings', put forward by Vyakarnam *et al*[5] in the 'Transitions' growth model. This argues that although the business will normally grow over time, and may do so either quickly or slowly, there are three recognisable levels and modes of operating a business.

---

5. Vyakarnam Jacobs & Pratten, This model will be enlarged in a subsequent book in this series *Planning for Growth*.

1. **Tactical**: focusing on daily survival, winning and fulfilling orders, and cash flow.
2. **Strategic**: when the business becomes more structured and plans carefully to achieve formal goals.
3. **Visionary**: in which the strong sense of shared purpose and cultural values permeate the business and people are coached and empowered to take action to realise the vision.

Any new venture will, at first, operate tactically, purely to survive. There may be a plan, a strategy, even a vision, but until the people in the business have learnt the survival skills, they are unlikely to have the 'headroom' to think and plan effectively.

The value of the 'glass ceilings' concept is that it helps to explain why most business ventures reach a point where they stop growing appreciably, and either plateau, continue to grow at a slow rate or decline. The 'glass ceiling' is the point at which the capabilities and experiences of the people running the business are fully stretched and they do not know how to 'do it better', because they have reached the limits of their learning. They can see through the glass ceiling that the business may have greater potential, but they cannot achieve it. A step change in the way the business operates needs to take place, to enable them to breakthrough the glass ceiling by working in a different way. The 'breakthrough' can only come as a result of learning to work differently, be it intentional or incidental, or of a change in personnel which introduces new thinking into the business.

Figure 4.3: The 'Transitions' glass ceilings model of growth[6]

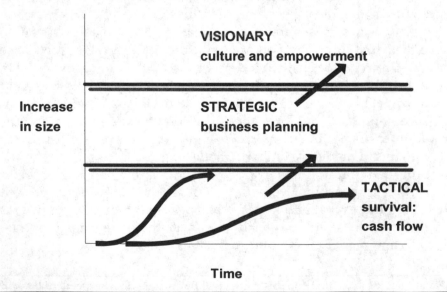

6. Vyakarnam, Jacobs & Pratten, *op.cit.*

In this way, the small business, typically five years after formation, may be very busy, working all hours to find new customers and to fulfil orders, stretching its resources of working capital, personnel and physical capacity to the limit – and, for those very reasons, unable to grow further. It is a common situation, where the only way forward is to learn how to manage the business differently. So finding new ways of understanding the position the business is in, and learning different ways of managing it, is vital for people to be able to grow their business.

Exercise
- Think of a business in which you have experience of working.
- Which level of growth – tactical, strategic or visionary – would you say it was in, and why?
- What factors needed to change in the business for it to grow beyond its glass ceiling?

WHAT IS GROWTH?

We must, in any case, ask the question of how best to measure the growth of a business. Sales turnover might be the most obvious, but it is not necessarily the most important, or universally relevant measure. Turnover may increase without profit increasing in proportion, or even at all. Below are some alternative factors that can be used to measure growth.

Financial	*Non-financial*
Increases in:	Increases in:
• gross profit margin;	• market share;
• net profit margin;	• number of customers, orders;
• dividend yield;	• number of employees;
• net asset value;	• number of outlets;
• share value;	• number of new products
• average spend per customer.	introduced.

Depending on the business, a combination of several of these may be more significant than a simple increase in sales turnover. Even then, they are of limited value in isolation. It really does matter what the rest of the industry, especially the competitors, are doing, and over what timescale. If a business in the IT service industry is growing its sales turnover at 15 per cent per annum against an industry average of 50 per cent, it is clearly underpeforming in relative terms. But is year-on-year growth of this magnitude sustainable for the industry? It could be that one firm is concentrating on a newly emerging, highly profitable technology and leaving the mass market to others. However, relating firm performance to competitive position is vitally important. Investors, customers, partners and employees will be attracted to successful, fast-growing businesses, and will be wary of slow-growing 'also-rans' if they seem to have had their day and are a potential target for customer raiding or acquisition.

Ultimately, however, how the success, performance and growth of a business are measured, through whatever combination of financial and non-financial factors, is a matter for the managers and investors in the business. We would expect the entrepreneurs and investors to have goals, targets and a strategy of some kind for the venture; to know what they want and have considered how best to achieve it. So the goals for different businesses in the same industry, which may even be in competition, could be as varied as the following.

- To be the industry leader, measured by market share and sales volume.
- To be the lowest cost producer and most profitable business.
- To develop a profitable niche business with a high asset value for sale within five years.
- To be the recognised technology innovator in the industry.
- To focus on the most profitable customers and to achieve the highest rate of profits growth.
- To develop a stable long-term customer base and yield a high rate of return for the investors.

Each of these is based on the positioning of the business in its market, together with the goals, capabilities and learning of the entrepreneurs. They are different, yet competing as one would expect.

Exercise
For the business venture you explored in Chapter 2:

- What goals would you set for the business (e.g. in the business plan)?
- What indicators would you use to measure its success?

THE ENTREPRENEURIAL PROCESS: FROM ENGAGEMENT TO EXIT

The simple 'life cycle' model of the business, of forming, surviving, growing and either continuing to exist or eventually disappearing through sale, merger or closure (which was discussed earlier in this chapter), predicts the trend of a business. It does not model the behaviour or involvement of the entrepreneur as the living agent who enacts the strategy. Since the entrepreneur and business are separate, with discrete if interconnected goals, the process through which the entrepreneur engages with the business needs to be considered.

The entrepreneur may form the business or they may enter at a later stage, for example as an employee, through acquiring the business, or by inheriting a family-owned business. Where the venture has a longer life than the duration of the entrepreneur's involvement with it, a process consisting of three recognisable stages can be identified: engaging with and entering the venture; working within it to achieve both business and personal goals; and finally moving out of the business. These stages are described more fully below.

Figure 4.4: The entrepreneurial process mapped onto the growth curve

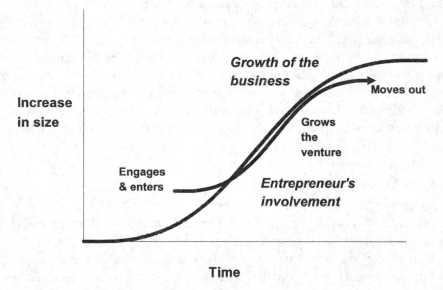

Engaging with and Entering the Venture

In a new venture, this may be through forming the idea and planning its creation, such as starting up or spinning out from a larger business. In the case of an existing business, it might include identifying it and assessing its potential as a buy-in. It is, essentially, an opportunity identification and evaluation stage, in which different options, possibilities and strategies may be examined before one is selected. It may take a matter of weeks or several years. Sometimes – as with the quest for a market opportunity for a start-up or a buy-in to an established business – the trail may be a long one with many disappointments before (if ever) the 'right combination' (however that is defined) comes along. Alternatively, the entrepreneur may have a firm goal of starting and running only one type of business, and sets about planning and starting it.

The point at which 'the rubber meets the road', is the moment when the entrepreneur actually starts a new business or assumes the control and some degree of ownership of a pre-existing venture. Chapter 5 explores this stage of the entrepreneurial process.

Growing the Venture

During this stage, the entrepreneur is committed to running the business, they are immersed in it and totally identified with it. They enact their own goals through their commitment to the venture, driving it forward, overcoming problems, creating and exploiting opportunities. They are the dynamic, energising force in the business. This is normally the longest stage and might well occupy most of the lifetime of the entrepreneur, although a recognisable group of 'serial entrepreneurs' will go into a new or existing business and seek to achieve rapid growth or a turnround before moving out. The entrepreneur is deeply engaged with the growth and success of the venture, sometimes even to the point of obsession; it is during this phase that they may feel that 'I am the business'. The challenges of survival, competition, growth and related business and personal issues will need to be resolved. There are many possible subsidiary stages and sub-processes within the phase, which will be considered in Chapter 6.

Moving Out and On

At some point, the entrepreneur disengages from the business and moves out. This can occur in different ways, and for differing reasons. Their departure may be planned, such as having a 5-year goal of retirement or sale of the business, or it may be unplanned and arise through circumstances such as ill health, a favourable offer to sell the business, or its failure. Equally, it may be voluntary or involuntary. It can be hard to move out, such is the emotional attachment and commitment made to the business, or it may be a relief. It may happen quickly, as in the case of sale or closure, or it may be a prolonged process of disengagement, such as an elderly parent gradually and reluctantly ceding control of a family business to their offspring. This is 'the dad problem' which children often experience in taking on the family business – dad (more rarely mum) does not know how or when to let go!

For many entrepreneurs, business life then continues – by starting or acquiring another business, or by becoming involved as an investor or non-executive director.

Just as the linear growth models can be criticised on the basis that they are not universally valid, so the process of entrepreneurial engagement with an enterprise is so diverse and varied in form, nature and duration that it can only be modelled in very general terms. However, this process of three phases, simplistic as it is, does relate to the reality of the experiences of very many entrepreneurs and it offers a way of making sense of their experiences, of following their story as distinct from the life cycle of a business venture. The following chapters, therefore, use this model to explore entrepreneurial experiences in the context of both the person and the business venture.

Most of us learn more readily from the experiences and stories of others than from theoretical models which, whilst they may distil broad research into a pure form, inevitably lose the authenticity and warmth of human experience which gives them meaning. The approach taken in the next three chapters is to follow a collection of entrepreneurial people through their experiences in launching and running their ventures, focusing through their narratives on the learning processes and development of strategies, capabilities and personal theories within each phase of the entrepreneurial process.

Each chapter is centred around three linked elements.

1. An initial discussion of the key questions associated with the start-up phase of the entrepreneurial process.
2. The stories of entrepreneurial people, exploring their experiences and insights around the 'growing' stage.
3. The themes and issues that emerge from their experiences, that help us to conceptualise, understand and apply the learning to our personal context.

CHAPTER 5

Engaging with and
Entering the Business

INTRODUCTION

This chapter is the first of three that follow the entrepreneur through the process of entering, growing and moving out of a venture. Its aim is to explore how people move into an entrepreneurial role, why they do so and to illustrate the varied forms which their ventures may take.

The approach which is taken in these chapters is to learn from the experiences of entrepreneurs in each phase through questioning and reflection. A series of themes is developed which enables us to conceptualise and make sense of the main issues and learning points in each chapter. There are many questions that arise in understanding and learning from people as they move into an entrepreneurial role. Initially, some overall and fundamental questions are posed and discussed briefly. These aim to stimulate you, as the reader, to reflect on your personal stance and also to think of the questions that interest you. Then the experiences of a group of entrepreneurs are related. The questions raised from the initial discussion can be used to explore and learn from these narratives. By reflecting on and considering both your personal stance and the wider experiences of others, the aim is that you can achieve useful insights into the process of engaging and entering a venture.

These are some of the key questions that could be asked of entrepreneurs in relation to their ventures.

- How and why did they select and engage with a particular venture?
- What was their aim?
- What was the 'fit' between the entrepreneur and the venture?
- Why did they think they could do better than people who were already doing it?
- What was the actual or potential opportunity they identified?
- Were they innovative?
- At what stage in their career did they engage with the venture?
- What form did the venture take?
- What and how did they learn in the process of engaging and entering?

How and Why did they Select and Engage with a Particular Venture?

People start, join or acquire businesses for many reasons. It seems that, very often, there is a combination of personal drive and ambition towards

a goal, together with a decision that the venture represents a better investment than other alternatives open to them, at that point in time.

The decision to enter a venture implies that a clear choice has been
made to do so. The choice may be only between the business and being
inactive, or it may be a choice between alternative business projects or
investments. The choices may have been conscious, rational and deliberate, which is what would be expected of business decisions.
However, the roles of unconscious choice, of an intuitive sense of direction, and of a process of emerging over time into an entrepreneurial
venture, may also be significant. In these ways, the individual may
achieve what they intended, without being fully aware of why they had
set out to do so or of the choices they had made.

What was their Aim?

The individual aims and aspirations together with the underlying motivations and driving forces are clearly of considerable significance in the
decision to enter a business venture. What did the individual expect to
gain? What were the connections between their motivations and the
selection of a particular venture as a way, quite possibly the way, of fulfilling them? Was it the desire to be wealthy, to be independent and 'in
control'? Was it the urge to own a stake in the business? Or was it self-
realisation through a particular project?

What was the 'Fit' between the Entrepreneur and the Venture?

Entrepreneurs can be characterised by such subjective attributes as their
experience and background, capabilities, expectations and goals, interests, likes and dislikes and their personality. Their prior experience and
learning, as well as their self-concept of 'the kind of person they are',
are likely to influence powerfully the nature of the business venture
they enter. The business itself can also be perceived in a number of
ways, including those shown in the opportunity assessment model in
Chapter 3, following the variables of investment, risk, return, change
and time. Other more specific factors are, however, likely to be important, including the product or service offered, the market (including
both customers and competitors), the process involved, the technology,
the people, current ownership, and past performance (if it is not a new
business) are all likely to play a part.

Somewhere in the relationship there are likely to be strong connections
between the person and the venture. In the case of someone succeeding
into a family business, these may seem to be obvious ties of family inheritance and loyalty, even though the management of family businesses
often does not pass to the next generation. Some further questions that
might be asked about the choice of a particular venture follow.

Why did they Think they could do better than People who were already Doing it?

Unless the business is based on an entirely new concept, it will either be a continuation of an existing business, for example by acquisition or inheritance, or a new entrant into an existing market. Either way, the entrepreneur presumably thinks they can 'squeeze more value' by achieving better results than those who are already in the market, by doing things differently or by managing more effectively.

What was the Actual or Potential Opportunity they Identified?

At the heart of the entrepreneurial process is the judgement by the entrepreneur that they have found a source of unrealised, or under-realised, value. This may be in a product, the market, in the business itself or in any combination of these. It may quite simply be in their own capabilities, which they think are undervalued as an employee and would be worth more in the open market. Their catalytic role is in unlocking and transforming this perceived undervaluing of an oppor-tunity into a real increase in value. Where the entrepreneur differs from the speculator is that they themselves act to realise the value rather than calculating that in time 'the market' will deliver an increase in value. However, in recognising this unexploited or underexploited source of value, the entrepreneur is seeing something that no one else has recognised or has thought worth trying to realise. It may be that the entrepreneur has seen it first or has judged that the time is likely to be right in terms of market conditions to exploit it.

Were they Innovative?

The opportunity may lie in some form of innovation; a new combination of previously known elements (as discussed in Chapter 3) or 'a new way of doing things'. The innovation may result in a completely new product, a new way of gaining access to a market, offering a product to a market which has not previously experienced it, or a process efficiency which enables a cost advantage to be gained over existing providers. Without some form of innovation to differentiate from established competitors, new ventures are likely to find it difficult to compete successfully.

At what Stage in their Career did they Engage with the Venture?

People may engage in entrepreneurial ventures at almost every stage in adult, and even pre-adult, life. The stage in their life, or indeed their career, when they do so may be significant. Why that venture and why at that moment? Was it their first entrepreneurial episode or part of an evolving pattern within their life story? There are people who started their first business venture in their youth, perhaps as an extension of a hobby or spare-time activity or as an alternative to paid employment. Others did so shortly after leaving college or university. A common career path is to gain several years of useful experience in working as an employee, attaining management or professional responsibilities, before venturing into an entrepreneurial career. This may come about through leaving paid employment, or through forming a spin-out business either backed by, or in competition with, the former employer. It may, alternatively, involve effectively taking control of some or all of the business and running it in an entrepreneurial way. There are many possible combinations. Finally, entrepreneurship may come about in mid or late-career, perhaps through early retirement, redundancy or choosing to pursue a different career agenda. This would include entrepreneurs who had grown a business successfully, sold it or moved into a non-executive role, and then take an interest in other businesses.

Whatever their career stage, what entrepreneurs were doing immediately prior to entering the venture is likely to be relevant. It may be that it was unsatisfactory for them, possibly unfulfilling, frustrating or unrewarding in some way. It may be that they had learned from it that they could do more, had outgrown the role, and moved on.

What Form did the Venture Take?

The range of possible modes for a venture is wide, and may include the following.

- Their own new start-up business.
- Forming a partnership or team-based business.
- Entering an existing business, e.g. as a manager or employee or as a buy-in.
- Taking on the management or ownership of an existing business, e.g. a family succession or buy-out.
- Buying a franchise.
- Buying a business which results from the divestment of non-core activity or outsourcing by a larger business.
- A spin out of a new opportunity from an existing business.
- Privatisation of a formerly publicly owned activity.

Again, there are many possible variations. The one which takes place may have been chosen by the entrepreneur or it may have become available and represented an attractive opportunity at the time.

What and How did they Learn in the Process of Engaging and Entering?

Entering a business venture can be an intense learning experience, especially when doing so for the first time. There are many new things that that it may be necessary to learn how to do. Former executives of large companies can be almost as disorientated and surprised by the range of tasks they are responsible for as much as a less experienced young person. Learning what to do, how to avoid failure and to get things right, initially how to survive and then to succeed, what the (unwritten) rules of the market are, and so on, are often key lessons.

Learning by experience is one – often hard – way; learning from other, more experienced people, from their advice and example, are powerful sources. However, the power and influence of prior learning is highly influential in affecting the perception, decision making and actions in this phase. From their prior and current experience, a range of what might be called 'how-tos' emerges; approaches which are found to work in a given set of circumstances, making sense of how they did it, problem solving, mistakes, failures, successes. As these are tested and found to be effective, they become 'tacit' and intuitive in use, and form part of the bank of learned behaviours and personal theories which are built up over life. Equally, prior learning may lead people to reject valuable ideas and approaches because they do not think they could be made to work; their prior learning represents a barrier to new thinking which may constrain the success of the business.

Exercise

Which questions would you add to those already discussed, which may help you to understand the process of engaging with and entering a venture?

Take a few minutes to reflect and note these down. Then read the entrepreneurs' narratives which follow with these questions in mind.

ENTREPRENEURS' LIFE STORIES

This chapter (together with the next two) is formed largely of the stories of how selected people developed their entrepreneurial careers. In every case, their achievements are real and substantive. Their stories are their own descriptions, in their own words, of what they did, how and why they did it. They form personal narratives of their histories. There are two important points concerning the interpretation and use of life stories in this way.

1. Each story is the individual's own narrative, a discourse concerning themselves, their past, present and future. Each story is influenced and formed by the teller's self-concept of their identity, their personality, their motivations and capabilities. It also includes their perceptions of events, their actions and achievements. By definition, they

are subjective accounts, which allow the reader to 'get under the skin' and gain insights into how the person thought, decided and acted. The stories are not objective, biographical case studies, but neither are they self-justifying or self-serving accounts. Each story offers a different perspective on the entrepreneurial experience, the way in which the teller matched their own driving forces and capabilities against the opportunities and challenges of the external world and worked towards realising their own aspirations.

2. The stories are told by people who, at the time of writing, were extremely active in business. Some, when interviewed, were building their first business, others were leading an established business on to renewal, further growth and success. Others again had moved out and on to play a different role as non-executive chairmen and directors of other businesses. All talked candidly about themselves and their experiences. In order to protect sensitivities and confidential aspects in relation to past and current relationships, their identities have been disguised by the use of a first name only. However, the reader should be assured that the identity is the only element that has been changed.

Entrepreneur	Occupational background	Nature of business venture
Claire	Personnel manager	Performance coaching
Anna	Computer sales	Computer services
Mark	Engineering quality assurance	Fabrication engineering
Brian	Retail, finance and sales	Equipment hire
Linda	Public service	Etching service
Barry	Engineering, photography	Etching service
John	Law	Retailing
Mike	Hotel and catering	Recruitment consultancy
David	Toy industry marketing	Child car-safety accessories
Robert	Chemistry	Food industry

Each story illustrates a different aspect of the phase of 'engaging and entering a venture'. Most of the entrepreneurs will reappear in the next chapters in which the subsequent phases of their ventures will be explored.

1. MOVING FROM A SENIOR MANAGEMENT ROLE INTO CREATING A NEW BUSINESS

Claire

Claire established her career in personnel management and over eighteen years worked in large retail and food organisations, progressively gaining senior level positions, then moved into health care.   Having built up a successful career as a personnel director, she decided to leave and start her own business in executive coaching and mentoring.

I have always broken the rules. I have never done anything dishonest, but I always remember my grandfather who gave me this advice: 'Ask yourself three questions: so what, who cares and what difference does it make? If you can't answer those you go on and do something else.' That has really been my philosophy.

I knew that I was not using my potential, quite simply I was doing a jolly good job and I was being paid an obscene amount of money. I had a great car and all the rest of it, and I thought, 'I could carry on doing this, retire at 55, I will look back and think what have done with my life, zip all really.' So it was about my own self-worth. I've never really considered myself to be entrepreneurial, but I knew that I could do a lot more, I don't really know what but to do it for me.

I left and I set up my own business, and that is my forte, working for me and generating income for me. It never occurred to me that I could not do it. That would be outside my realm of thinking. From a very early age it has always been instilled in me. I know I can do anything I want to do even now, and I have never really asked myself before, I just know.

I used my contacts, I contacted everybody I knew. I said, 'I'm working for myself, I know I can help you, what have you got for me?' I never ever felt any shame. I am very well connected, if I met somebody I kept their business card and I've made a point of always remembering everybody's name. I use a lot of mind mapping skills and rapport, so I will always have something to ring them over. So that is how I started, cold calling, ringing up people, but not just 'Hi what you can give me?' I ring up and say, 'I have found the most incredible culture change stuff', and who is ever going to say 'No', nobody really, so that is the way I went about it.

In Claire's story of her disengagement from an executive career and engagement with her own venture, there is a strong sense of lack of fulfilment and absence of meaning in working even at a senior level in corporate organisations. She had a powerful motivation to realise her potential by creating her own venture, which would use her skills and reward her by making a difference to her clients. She recognised an opportunity to apply psychological techniques in executive and sports coaching and mentoring to help individuals, teams and organisations to improve their performance. Significantly, her business did not take the form of a myriad of other small consultancies. Within five years of starting, she had grown a client base of leading corporate and sporting organisations, with a network of facilitators running over 200 events each year and with annual fee income of several million pounds.

2. MOVING FROM RUNNING SOMEONE ELSE'S BUSINESS INTO YOUR OWN

Anna

Anna left school at sixteen and started working as a secretary in a computer company. Coming from what she describes as *'a very working class, ordinary background'*, her biggest motivation was *'to go out and earn money, that's all I ever saw myself doing. I wanted to earn lots of money. It was greed if you like, because I've always wanted the nice things in life. I thought I'm going to get those and I made myself go out and become successful in my own right because what I wanted to have didn't come naturally to me'*.

She developed skills in wordprocessing and became an expert in wordprocessing systems, then progressed to demonstrating and selling those systems to clients. She became confident and successful in selling, and joined a family-owned computer business as sales manager. The founder died, leaving the business to his family but with Anna now running it successfully.

Suddenly I had this business to run which employed ten people, turning over about £400,000 and it was a major panic, where did I go, what did I do? It was suddenly left to me, his children left it all totally in my control and they wanted me to run it and look after it straight away, of course they got the money for it. I was just a manager at that stage, and I had to learn very quickly, I learnt through journals, experience, gut feeling, ended up reading all sorts of text books relating to finance, motivation skills and transferable skills. After about three years I entered the 'Business Woman of the Year Award' and won. It gave me so much confidence because I turned the business from a £400,000 into a £2 million turnover business, and at that stage I was still working for somebody else.

I could see how much money I was making for other people who were not directly involved in the business and I thought 'I am this business, this business is me'. I had no children, no family, nothing to lose.

I decided then I wanted to go on my own. I knew I could, I believed in myself, I had proven to myself that I could do it. I went to ask the family, the owners of the company if I could become a shareholder and they said 'No'. I was actually making too much money for them. They would give me an increase in salary to stay with them, but they did not want to give up any shares so I thought, 'Right I will go on my own.' I looked around for somebody to go into business with me for, although I had the confidence, I did not have the finance behind me. I also found a computer business in the Midlands who were looking at opening another office and who wanted to go into partnership with me.

So I went into partnership. I set up a very small office with three people, two of whom were from my previous company, who were my technicians. I became the sales person and they were the people who went out

*and installed the products and services for me. I found that the customer
base I had before was very loyal to me and they followed me. We never
ever went into a loss, we were immediately in profit but we were almost
over-trading because we were so successful in a short space of time.*

In Anna's story, there is a theme of a person who was highly determined and driven to make money and to be successful. Having left
school as quickly as she could, she regretted it, but found she could
learn by doing, from other people and by studying on her own. She
developed through experiential learning the capabilities of presenting,
selling, leading others and inspiring successful performance. In working her way from secretary to manager, she gained confidence until she
reached the point of realising that she wanted more and was worth
more than the business employing her was prepared to give.

This point, the realisation of one's own worth, the feeling of being
undervalued in a career and the need to be valued and recognised to
the full, is a crucial one for many entrepreneurs. The wish to move
from paid employee – even as a highly paid manager – to having a
stake of the equity, a share in the ownership of the business, is often an
acid test, a 'moment of truth' for the entrepreneurial spirit. In neither
Claire's nor Anna's stories were they insecure, under threat of redundancy, or financially under-rewarded – yet there was something missing which was so important to them that they walked out of a highly
paid executive careers to go and create the business which embodied
their abilities and values. Each of them took what might be considered
a big risk, yet they were completely confident that they would be more
successful and would gain the satisfaction of owning their business.

It so happens that both Anna and Claire are female entrepreneurs.
They are both successful, extremely focused on what they want and determined to achieve it. They have worked extremely hard, and have also
had children and have maintained family relationships along the way. As
two individuals, they probably have few shared characteristics other than
these. Traditionally, there have been fewer female than male entrepreneurs, certainly in the UK. For years, people such as Dr Steve Shirley,
who founded the FI Group in 1963, or the high-profile Anita Roddick who
co-founded The Body Shop, were regarded as unusual, counter-typical
examples. That is changing, and it is changing quickly. Growing numbers of women are realising that they can achieve independence and success through their own business ventures. They realise that this does not
have to involve the trade-off and compromise between having a family
and a corporate career which large organisations even now seem to
demand. There will be many more female entrepreneurs in the early
years of the 21st century, and the move towards creative, knowledge and
network based organisations is creating ever more opportunities for this.

3. REALISING AN AMBITION: FROM BEING AN EMPLOYEE TO STARTING A BUSINESS

Mark

The next story is, again, a person who felt he could achieve more in his own business than by working for others. Mark and a partner formed an engineering business in 1985. Mark's background was in engineering quality assurance and he identified an opportunity to supply stainless steel fabrication services to food and other companies that needed high purity process equipment. Initially, Mark and his partner worked on a self-employed basis and rented workshop space and the facilities from another fabrication business to do subcontract work.

> *I was working for an engineering moulding company. I put myself back into college, got off the shop floor and I became a quality assurance inspector at a local company, which did a lot of work for the nuclear industry. It was whilst I was working there that me and my partner had this ambition to start in business on our own. We always had it and the idea was to have a small engineering company that offered the services and the quality assurance capabilities of the bigger companies at a more competitive price.*
>
> *At first we could not get started, but we had the opportunity to do some security railings and guards for a local company. We basically went self-employed and used the guillotine and equipment in the shop to grow our own business, which was an ideal opportunity for us. So whilst we were doing this work, I was ringing round other companies to try and get work from them. Consequently, when we started we had about £200 in the bank, we were surviving on the bare minimum and we built the business up to a point where the work that I was getting in was more than this other chap was giving us. So we outgrew the premises that he was renting to us to do his work and we moved to premises which were about 3,000 square feet at the time.*

Mark's story is one of being clear about the eventual goal of setting up an engineering business to meet a specific need in the market place and to run the business to high quality standards. Mark was aware that he did not have all the skills required to establish the business and spent several years preparing and putting the different elements in place by getting the training he needed, finding workshop space and equipment to use, and once he and his partner had become self-employed, selling their services to customers to build up the level of work to achieve viability and to start to fulfil the original vision. Initially they were '*ducking and diving*', putting everything back into the business to finance its growth. His own background in quality assurance is reflected in the aims and values of the business and the determination to achieve the ISO 9000 certification for the quality assurance system. Mark's story is also originally about a partnership business, but the relationship did not survive the dynamics of growing the business.

Me and my partner fell out, as partnerships do go that way, there's always a stronger partner comes out. It always seems to be the way so, consequently, I bought Chris out and went it alone.

4. AN ENTREPRENEURIAL TEAM STARTS AN ENTIRELY NEW TYPE OF BUSINESS
Brian

The stories of engagement and entry cited so far have been for businesses based very much on the founders' skills, their expertise and background having enabled them to identify market opportunities for selling their capabilities. The next account, which centres on Brian, is different in two significant respects. The business he co-founded was one in which he had no prior experience whatsoever. Also, it was a business venture started by a team of three rather than a sole entrepreneur or a partnership of two. Brian had started his career firstly in selling advertising space in magazine publishing, in which he had developed a confident and successful approach to selling.

My father said 'you are a born salesman, therefore you should be a salesman', but you can apply sales ability or engaging personality in so many ways. You don't have to be a salesman.

Brian joined the family finance company in the 1960s, which provided hire purchase and rental facilities for electrical goods retailers. Whilst he was successful in growing its profitability six-fold, he identified a threat to the business in the form of the then new credit card format, which he foresaw would decimate small hire purchase companies. He identified the need to do something else and together with two friends experimented with various ideas and hit on an opportunity to hire power tools and equipment to builders.

The person who shared a flat with my colleague worked for a builders' merchant and said to him, 'there might be a business in hiring our paint sprays'. He knew someone who owned a paint spray and builders kept asking if they could borrow it. The finance company lent them the money to buy the first paint spray and that's how we started. There was no tool hire in this country in 1965, we started in 1971 which was the classic date to start and by 1975 the industry was in full swing.

It was quite obvious from day one that people wanted to hire the stuff. One of us worked for a builders' merchant and was quite mechanically switched on, the other is an accountant and I am entre-

preneurial – all three of us were entrepreneurial actually, and I am not thick where mechanical things are concerned. I can remember when I was fourteen or fifteen I used to love fiddling around with my bike and I realised that to do jobs on your bike took hours and I thought if I get too carried away doing that I'm not going to make any money.

The business was quickly successful, partly through having the right product at the right time, but also to a large degree through innovative marketing. Brian conceptualised the essentials of the business format in his mind and devised the idea of a catalogue, which was designed to market the business, that builders or anyone in industry could keep on site and quickly identify the tools they needed, then collect them from a local branch. The whole business formula was designed in this way, offering the customer a completely new service that was convenient to use.

I personally was a pioneer, and I thought 'What is this business about? It is about getting items of equipment to people who will use them to make their lives easier.' To do that, the major thing is you're not selling tools, you are selling a leaflet that tells people how their lives can be easier. I thought, 'How do we do that?' Firstly you have to get your name across, so that when a prospective customer picks it up he must at a glance be able to tell what any item of equipment is, what it does, what it looks like and what it costs. Our first catalogue was really so similar to today's beautiful colour catalogue, nearly 30 years on, it is amazing. That became the bible of the entire industry in this country, and it was me who devised it.

The business was built on solid marketing and selling, establishing a customer base, providing what they wanted, when they wanted it.

The whole thing was a marketing exercise up to a point, I would go onto building sites in the very early days and say, 'Here is our catalogue, a building site is not complete without one of these'; and that was before other people did it. When we started to get competition, I used to go to trading estates with my salesman and go into every single warehouse or office, every single one, and say, 'Have one of our new catalogues, you may not need it this week or even this month but I can guarantee that before this year is out you will need some equipment from us, so keep this catologue for when the time comes.' The whole business was built upon doing a little bit of business with lots of people, because tool hire is one of those things that you don't need all the time.

5. SEEING 'A WAY OF DOING IT BETTER'

Rather than offering a completely new service proposition, as the tool hire business did, a frequently adopted strategy is to identify a mismatch between the service offered by existing operators and the service levels which customers expect or would prefer. The business then offers 'a better way of doing things' in the industry than established competitors and can attract their customer base. The following example is a business that also offered a fairly new process technology in metal etching which had the potential for much wider adoption.

The Etched Products Business

The business was formed in 1990 by Bob, Barry and Linda. Bob was working as a sales manager for an etching company and was frustrated by the poor customer service it offered, Barry had expertise in engineering and photography. Recognising the potential of the etching process and the scope for providing much better customer service than existing firms, they set up the business. Barry, the managing director, explained how the company has developed.

The idea for the business came from Bob who had been working for an etching company as a sales manager, but there were very few etching companies in the UK, and its customer service was abysmal. The company's attitude to the customer was 'you'll get it when we say', its delivery time was normally six weeks or more. They all had very much the same attitude because they were all tarred with the same brush, and it was a limited market as far as the customer was concerned. So Bob was getting kicked because he wasn't getting new customers, but all the time he was going round pacifying the ones he'd got trying to keep them, and he felt he was bashing his head against a brick wall. The company I worked for was taken over by an etching company but I left because of the politics.

I had once said to Bob, 'You know all about etching, why don't you start on your own?' It seems very simple, very basic, although there is a lot more to it than meets the eye. After about a year we met again at an exhibition and he said to me he was thinking of going on his own and I said I would like to go in with him, and that was it. About three months later we started. The basic aim of the company was to give customer service. Initially we halved everyone else's lead times because we could not see why it was six weeks, three weeks was perfectly adequate. Our whole ethos was to keep the customer informed, sometimes you are going to let the customer down because you are reliant on a lot of other things. So what we do is phone the customer and let them know as soon it is going to be available and, even today, that absolutely floors them.

6. ENTERING THE FAMILY BUSINESS

The businesses described so far have all been new ventures, yet it should not be assumed that entrepreneurship is always necessarily about starting a new business. The value locked up in existing businesses, of differing sizes and ages, can provide many ways for a person to develop an entrepreneurial approach, and several of these will feature in this, and subsequent, chapters.

Family owned businesses make up the vast majority of smaller businesses. The phrase 'from clogs to clogs in three generations' described the way in which a business set up by a hard-working person from a poor background was handed on to subsequent generations who mismanaged and squandered the assets, resulting in a return to poverty. This might be an extreme case, but it does illustrate two of the often-linked dilemmas of family businesses. Firstly, there is the question of who can, and does, succeed to the ownership and management of the business, and whether they have the capabilities and motivation to be successful and are allowed to do so by the family. Secondly, there is the problem of renewing the business so that it does not stagnate or become regarded purely as a 'cash cow' by the non-working shareholders.

Moving into a management role in a family business is often a peculiar mix of learning the personalities, norms and even rituals of the ways things are done. The experience may be quite different for someone who is born into the family, who may know what to expect, as opposed to 'an outsider' who enters as an employee.

The example, which we will follow, is a retailing business, founded by two brothers. The entrepreneur, John, married into the family, after training as a lawyer. He describes his entry and early experiences in the business.

I did the usual things that you do when you go into a family business, which is to work in every single department. It was a complete and utter waste of everyone's time, particularly mine, because I got very bored very quickly and everybody jostled to explain that you don't know what you are doing.

I was very fortunate that I worked for the two founders, brothers who were highly intelligent. They were extremely focused on what each of them, independently, was doing. One was the merchandiser, he totally and utterly concentrated on that and the other was the financial controller and administrator of the business who completely focused on that. They brought a high degree of intelligence, drive and enthusiasm to everything they did. I learnt a tremendous amount from them in that context. It was not formal learning, it was very much watching the way in which they behaved. They were both very hard with the people who worked for them, but were also tremendously charismatic and the people working for them absolutely adored them. I found it amazing to see the way in which, on the one hand, they could be so adored, and on the other hand they could be so brutal with the same people, but nevertheless it worked.

I became bored very quickly and I was extremely fortunate to come across an outside, non-executive director of the business, a solicitor who was brilliant in his commercial understanding. He taught me everything I know about how to control a business and to make decisions and the need to implement those decisions and never ever to duck them. That was a tremendously difficult thing to learn, because there is always a very good excuse for not doing something. He made me understand that if you analyse the problem, you identify the solution, then you really have to go all the way to implement it.

This brought me back to what I had realised from the two brothers, their tremendous focus and determination. I think that is what differentiates an entrepreneur from an ordinary executive. The buck always stops with you, you identify the problem, you initiate the solution and you actually achieve it and it's the determination to do that and do it quickly and effectively. Very often with that determination, you are being prepared to be unpopular whatever comes.

John's narrative describes ways in which the approaches to managing and directing the business were modelled by the existing directors and were available for him to learn from. In turn, he was able to incorporate what he perceived as the successful aspects into his own approach to running a business. The results of this learning may be assessed from his description of how he was later invited to take control of the business.

The company got into a mess because of the family's involvement and I was asked by the outside director effectively to take control of the business and to put it right. I felt it was impossible because I identified that the family was the problem and I identified the solution, which was to get rid of the family. I didn't think it was possible, but having been taught the lesson I implemented it, I did get rid of the family, it was extremely successful and that was probably the greatest lesson I ever learned. I was in my early thirties, dealing with strong and powerful personalities in a very highly emotional atmosphere, but it worked extremely well. To the very great credit of the two brothers, they accepted that what I did was necessary and was done properly.

The next thing was to put the business right, and I accepted my weakness was that, although a good financial man and motivator of people, I was not a merchandiser and any retail company needs a merchant. So I identified the best in the country and I went out and I set the chap on. I didn't care what I had to do, he had to start. To achieve this I gave him my word that there would be no further interference by the family. Now it was that ruthlessness, that determination and that focus that achieved what we set out to achieve. We divided the areas of responsibility very clearly between us and that enabled him to get on with what he wanted to do and we then had ten years of tremendous success.

THEMES WHICH EMERGE FROM THE STORIES

Here we look for the themes and meanings that emerge from these narratives: what can we learn about the processes of engaging and entering a venture from these experiences?

Selecting the Venture

Most of the people whose stories are included in this chapter, formed a venture around an activity in which they were already involved. Whether they were in engineering, computer services, or personnel development, they used the skills and expert knowledge they already possessed as the basis for their business. They already understood the technology and the marketplace. Crucially, they felt they could they could do it better than it was already being done, and do it for themselves.

Two of the people had a different experience. They did not have direct experience in the particular industry they wished to enter, but were able to transfer their skills and expertise from one context to another. Brian's creativity and flair for sales translated from a finance business, through a series of experiments, into equipment hire. John's story is of a long induction into a family business and a process of learning about running businesses.

The opportunities identified by each person are interesting. Those in the engineering field – Mark and Barry – saw the potential for a firm to offer a better service to the industry than was currently available. Customer service and value would make their businesses distinctive and enable them to develop a customer base by giving a better service. Brian created and pioneered an entirely new service concept through visualising the tool hire firm based on a catalogue and hire depots, again, making it easy for the customer to buy, so selling the service effectively into the industry. Claire had identified an opportunity for a high level coaching and performance enhancement business.

In each case, a source of value was identified which was being underexploited, if exploited at all. Businesses would pay for tool hire, or for a better etching or fabrication service. In each case, they entered the business at a particular time, both in their careers and in terms of the market opportunities. They matched their judgement about the opportunity for unlocking value with the market situation that existed at the time. Their reasons for entering a business at that particular time were personal, driven by their own motivations and affected very much by 'the situation' rather than identifying the best possible moment to do so. Rather than perfect timing, it seems to have been about designing the concept that was the best one to meet the opportunities they perceived.

Motivations

There was a range of motivations for entering the different ventures. Frustration with the current situation – for them personally, or with the way things were done in the industry – was a powerful factor for several people. Anna and Claire had proved their effectiveness in top management roles, but wanted to run their own business. The desire for equity and to be an owner of a business – even a part owner – rather than an employee is extremely strong. There is a sense of disillusionment in working hard for other people, whether a family business or a large plc, and being rewarded but nevertheless feeling that 'I am worth more than this'.

The close personal identification with the business – as Anna said, '*I am this business, this business is me*' – is significant. If the business and the person driving it are felt to be one and the same, ownership by a third party does not fit. The personal commitment and drive invested by the entrepreneur is so great that they have to feel that it is their business. The need for control and independence – as Mark said, '*we had this ambition to start in business on our own*' – is a strong one.

Wanting the material rewards from business success, wanting to be wealthy is, not surprisingly, highly important for most. They want to make money and are prepared to be totally committed to the business in order to do so. Their reasons for wanting to be wealthy are more varied. Childhood and family background plays a large part for some. Wanting to have money and an enjoyable lifestyle when you felt disadvantaged as a child, or being very aware of parents' expectations that you make your way in the world, can be an important factor.

Other People

Most, though not all, of the entrepreneurs involved other people in entering the business. Brian's story (together with that of Linda, Barry and Bob) is an example of a new business started by an entrepreneurial team rather than a lone entrepreneur. Mark's business also started originally with a partner. There are sometimes tensions within these arrangements, which may cause them to become counter-productive or to fail. In Anna's story, she was the prime mover who gathered a team of known, reliable and compatible people around her to establish the venture, whilst forming a partnership with an existing business. There is a feeling that none of these people wanted to or at the time felt they could do it entirely on their own. There was a series of choices – partly deliberate, partly emergent – around building the team for the venture.

Learning

Finally, each of the people had learned a great deal about business before they moved into a prime role as entrepreneur. Working within the industry, learning from other people as well as from personal experience, and consciously developing their skills, characterise these personal journeys. There is a sense of preparing for entrepreneurship in several of the stories – in going back to college, in gaining high-level experience within leading companies, in almost serving an apprenticeship within a family business of which they must either take control or move out. There is a process of personal growth over time, as both self-confidence as well as capability are developed. There are figures from which they learn and whose influence is pivotal, but they tend not to be cited as role models. Finally, there is the development of personal theories which give them the acuity to be able to run their businesses effectively.

REVIEW

Go back to the questions you wanted to ask about engaging with and entering the venture. From the entrepreneurs' stories and the discussion of the themes that emerge, what are your conclusions to these questions?

Two in-depth studies of entrepreneurs moving into businesses close this chapter. These demonstrate the application of the entrepreneurs' personal learning to the processes of entering a business. The first study is of Mike, following his journey into starting his own business. The second is of David, who undertakes a buy-out of an existing business.

1. ESTABLISHING A NEW BUSINESS
Mike

Mike established a recruitment and human resources consultancy, absorbing the business he had run as a partnership for the previous year. His vision was *'to become established in the recruitment industry by providing a professional service for clients to achieve maximum efficiency, building on relations and forming partnerships'*.

The aim of the business was to provide a total human resource service, focusing on recruitment of permanent staff within three occupational sectors: IT, sales and commercial. The services provided by the consultancy included:

- search and selection;
- temporary personnel;
- handling responses to media adverts;
- career assessment and advice service;
- outplacement;

- psychometric testing;
- consultancy.

Operating in the fiercely competitive recruitment industry, the business aimed to differentiate itself from recruitment agencies and 'head-hunters' by offering a full range of services, by arranging bespoke services for clients and by providing a personal, relationship-based service to clients. The business established a consistent formula, which meant that, once it proved successful, it could be expanded rapidly by opening new offices. An ambitious growth plan was developed, including opening three further branches over the following two years. This is Mike's story of how he came to launch his business.

Early life and career formation

I went to grammar school, and when I left I decided I wanted to go into catering, and looked for college opportunities. But my parents wanted me to get out to work straight away, so I started work in a training scheme in a vegetable nursery, then in an estate agent's office as a sales negotiator until the office closed. I ended up getting a job with McDonald's and, after six months as a catering assistant, I was promoted to floor manager. At the age of eighteen I was asked to leave due to not being capable of managing people.

I started employment with Little Chef in 1984 as a general assistant, then over a $4^{1}/_{2}$ year period rose to supervisor, deputy manager, until finally I was the youngest manager employed in one of their roadside restaurants which involved a variety of tasks, recruiting, training, interviewing, customer service, and so on.

I turned the round restaurant that I was managing and achieved 23 per cent net profit. I was then promoted to general manager on a bigger site with a restaurant and a lodge-type hotel. Two years later, I moved again to a bigger site. Again, it was very much a hands-on position, requiring a lot of delegation and development of supervisors into managers.

In over ten years I developed many supervisors, deputy managers and branch managers, through training and showing them the skills and experience they would need to run a successful restaurant. I learnt a lot from my last Area Manager. She was very focused on what she needed to achieve, and used systems, but she also delegated budgetary control to her managers, which developed them and increased their financial awareness. I've proved it worked in everything I've set up here. You need to have a system and then to be prepared to change it to make it work better. That's where I got a lot of ideas regarding the systems I practise. I learned a lot from her, plus I learned a lot from Forte on man-management and sales, so it was a good base for me to learn. However, I left when my position was made redundant along with other managers when everyone had to re-apply for their jobs.

Changing career direction

I was in a difficult situation as to what to do next, so I registered with a recruitment agency and I was put straight out onto an assignment. At that point a lot was going on in my personal life, including divorce proceedings. I was left alone with a large house and needed money coming through the door so I thought 'how am I going to pay for this?' I took up a part-time telesales job in the evenings in double-glazing and also a part-time bar job at the weekends as well as working full-time Monday to Friday. I knew that to get into recruitment you needed telesales experience, and I knew double-glazing telesales was easy to get into so that was one reason I got the part-time job. I suppose, even at that point, I had a view of what I wanted to do in the future. I knew I could do the job, it was just proving to people that I could do it. I'm a great believer that anyone can do the basics of a specific job but you need the skills to back it up. I stuck it out for a year and proved I could get over it. I don't want to be in that position again but if I am I will go and take a job in a bar, I won't be 100 per cent happy but I will do it, that's the mentality I have.

With the telesales experience I got into temporary recruitment in Manpower. I was looking after driving personnel, supplying HGV drivers. Because of my flexibility, I'd go in at weekends and work late in the evenings. I turned the business round by obtaining the drivers and made it the most successful desk in an individual branch. I learnt a lot from Manpower, which is one of the industry leaders in recruitment.

Forming a business venture

It was obvious that the opportunities in recruitment were out there and I knew that I could do the job. I ended up working for a company as a recruitment consultant. Whilst doing this job, I was again achieving targets, recruiting personnel, finding people the right jobs for the right career. I'd often thought, 'Why am I doing this for a company? I could be doing it for myself?' At that point a colleague approached me and said, 'Have you ever thought of setting up by yourself?'

I set up in business with him, the reason we set it up was that there was no specific recruitment company just looking after permanent recruitment. With the skills and experience we had both learned from the recruitment industry, we thought 'the clients deserve a better service' but no one was actually giving it to them, it was just keeping them on the register until something came along.

We had no capital and we set up with a £4,000 overdraft. Running your own company is a bigger shock to the system when you've got no capital and you're always thinking, 'Hold on, am I doing the right thing?' It's not easy and at the time we stuck to three types of vacancies and we had no other services to offer.

We took on board another consultant to look after executive recruitment and an administrator. Again we were naïve, we didn't know about the legal implications of employing people but once they're on board you start to realise there are laws regarding employing people. On my return from holiday, I put it to the other partner that I couldn't work with him because after the first twelve months of trading we turned over £70,000 and lost £17,000. I felt that the commitment was not there from him when it was there from myself. After a lot of discussion, he said the only option was for me to buy him out.

Taking control of the business

So in the end, I bought my ex-partner out. The financial manager of one of our clients gave me a lot of input on how to run the business, being a qualified accountant helped and he ended up joining the business. I set up on my own as a sole trader, relocated to bigger premises with two employees, a recruitment consultant, and administrator and myself taking a hands-on approach. I soon realised I should take a hands-off approach; it turned out to be more beneficial for me to manage because that's what I'm good at, focusing on what we need to achieve rather than the day to day running.

Growth strategy

The business volume started to increase, we set targets and budgets and recruited another two consultants. At this point we also looked to the total HR solutions market, covering seven services which no other recruitment company covered. These were proving to be very effective with existing clients but we needed to push them more with future clients.

When we looked at operating businesses, whatever the size of company, in over 90 per cent of them there would be an IT division, a sales department and a commercial division – we homed in on those three sectors, plus offering all the services behind them as well. Once we'd got that strategy set in place and trained into the consultants the business started to grow very quickly. Our target is now for £250,000 turnover and we are on line to make a profit of 18 per cent as opposed to a deficit last year.

The consultants we've employed are clearly focused, they have experience in their sectors and are trained in the way we operate. We've moved forward, I have a better direction and we have a financial director who also knows where we are going. Because the strategy worked so successfully and we started seeing a return within the first three months of the consultants joining, we then looked forward to opening our second office. We lost three consultants in a short space of time and that put things back a few months. The new office opened with the same philosophy of IT, sales and commercial markets and it is now successfully mak-

ing a profit, as is our first office, which is achieving its target and mak-ing a profit. Our next office is due to open in three months, again the same formula will be applied, the same sectors, the same strategy. The consultants start on a probationary period of three months and they're not targeted until their third month, therefore, all the costs are planned up front. We plan to open two more offices within fifteen months, we've already started making inroads into those areas.

Financial targets and systems

The business has always been financed by self-generated investment, with no inward investment. For a business to operate on a £4,000 over-draft for the first couple of years is pretty good. The reason it's been suc-cessful is that my personnel come first when taking a salary and I come last and take out my salary as and when I need it. If it wasn't for the consultants, we wouldn't be successful, but I look at it another way: if I didn't have the strategy, the vision or the commitment or the control or the management, then the business wouldn't exist anyway.

I designed the business in my mind; it's looking at systems, seeing how they work and trying them. The systems we've got have all been devel-oped and implemented by myself. Profit is a key factor but if you haven't got systems in place, if you haven't got management controls and skills, if you haven't got a theory or a direction then the profit won't be there. You need systems – stick to the systems and manage to those systems, then have the flexibility to deviate from them. Providing you've got all of those key areas, the business will inevitably make a profit.

Everyone in the business knows about control, everyone has their own budget, everyone knows what profit they're expected to make each week and each month. They all see their targets on a daily or weekly basis, they see them increasing, they have incentives on a monthly and 6-monthly basis, they have an excellent bonus scheme. Everyone needs money, as long as we make a profit and achieve the target for the next quarter.

Managing people to achieve results

I'm a very good man-manager, so I utilise those skills to the best of my ability and train and develop the people around me so that they can identify their skills and utilise them in different areas of their ability. I look for certain qualities in people when recruiting.

What works for me is having the ability to encourage and develop people around me and point out the benefits to those people. If I see the people around me doing well, I know I'm going to do well. When I'm managing people and having weekly meetings with them, I identify their achievements and objectives for the next week. It allows me to identify any shortfall areas, which can be acted upon immediately as opposed to letting them brew. If I have a problem with somebody, I will talk to them about it and I will expect them to be as honest with me as I am with them.

At the end of the day there is no barrier between employee and employer, it's very much a teamwork environment, that's how it will stay. Because we are so small, we don't plan on having any more than one consultant for each centre, that provides the personal service to each client.

Personal goals and motivation

Why did I go into business on my own? It's something that I always wanted to do. Three years ago I didn't know what I wanted to achieve, all I would say was that I wanted to run my own business. Achieving sales targets motivated me, but only because I knew I could do it and to prove it. It's the people around me who motivate me, helping others to achieve and if they're doing it for the business they're doing it for me.

In five years time, I want to be able to retire, to have built a business that is not only profitable but also reputable in the industry. Not to retire and give up, I'll probably not move out of recruitment altogether, but to have the facility to retire and keep my hand in. But I also recognise the people behind me, and I know if the business is sold, I must have the ability and negotiating skills to say if I sell, these people stay with the company.

A lot of what drives me is pride, I don't like to be unsuccessful at anything I do. Being realistic is important, no one likes to fail, it's having the realism to think, 'Hold on a minute, if it does fail what are you going to do?' I have commitment, definitely 100 per cent commitment, if not more so. I am self-motivated to a degree, but also it's not putting that across to the employees, it's motivating them rather than my self-motivation. Also communication, organisation, and the determination to think that I'm not going to lose, I'm not going to drop out, I will succeed – and I will!

Questions to Consider in Relation to Creating a New Venture

- What characteristics of a new venture are likely to give it the best prospects for success?
- What factors are most likely to result in the business failing?
- What factors do you think differentiate a new venture with significant growth potential from one that is less likely to grow?

2. BUYING A BUSINESS: FROM EXECUTIVE TO ENTREPRENEUR

The Story of a Management Buy-in

This profile follows a senior executive who decided to fulfil an ambition by moving from a corporate career to acquiring a business through a management buy-in. It brings together the themes of selecting the venture, the entrepreneur's motivations, and the role of other people in an entrepreneurial team. It also focuses on unlocking the potential of an existing business that is run along traditional lines. The entrepreneur applies professional management approaches, which he has learned during his career in corporate business. Finally, it also touches on the use of a network of professional contacts – including an intermediary, accountants and lawyers, a venture capital investor and a chairman – to support the entrepreneur's endeavour.

A management buy-in (MBI) may occur where an entrepreneur identifies an underperforming or undervalued business with substantial potential for increasing its value. The aim is, normally, to grow and sell the business within three to five years. Generally, venture capital investors finance a MBI, enabling the entrepreneurs to buy a slice of the equity on more advantageous terms than the venture capitalists, in return for the capabilities they bring to the deal. There is a high attrition rate of potential MBIs – many things can go wrong in the processes of negotiation, the due diligence over the details of the business, the financing of the acquisition, and so on. An MBI normally involves a number of players; the entrepreneur(s), the investors, professionals, such as accountants and lawyers, and the vendor, all of whom have different interests and expertise and who must be able to co-operate for the MBI to succeed.

The Prime Mover and the Team

The leading figure was David, who had worked at senior management level in the toy industry, having achieved a track record of building high profit levels and adding substantial value to the businesses he had run. Having benefited from a takeover, David, who *'always had an ambition to run my own business and wanted to own my own company next time round'*, started looking for opportunities. He contacted an intermediary, the Chief Executive's Office, which is the focal point of a network of directors, business angels, institutional venture capital providers, and facilitates introductions between potential MBI and MBO candidates, vendors of businesses, and investors.

MBI candidates come under close scrutiny covering all aspects of their track record, management calibre, financial commitments and ability to make an equity investment in a business, since they form a vital part of the investment proposition. But the intermediary was convinced, at the end of a gruelling interview, that David was a *'driven, honest, hard-working and thoroughly professional MD who had what it takes'*.

The intermediary matched him with an experienced chairman who would take a non-executive role in the acquired venture and counter his lack of buy-in experience. He also met and vetted Alistair, the proposed sales and marketing director, who had gained top-level experience in selling and marketing. Together, they made a highly credible team, which would win the support of investors and be taken seriously by vendors.

The next stage was finding a business to acquire. The normal search process is to approach companies to explore their interest in divesting non-core divisions. It is advisable to have several – even as many as five – simultaneous lines of enquiry open, to provide the maximum opportunities and to be able to select the optimum investment with some objectivity. If there is only one option on the table, there is a danger, like Everest, of doing the deal 'because it's there'.

The Opportunity

The chairman of an investment company had indicated some time previously that he was interested in disposing of one of its businesses. The firm was a long established manufacturer of children's car safety seats and related accessories.

The business had an instant synergy with David's toy industry background and he saw the potential for adding-on toy offers to enhance the value of the car seat product. Since in-depth understanding of the market sector is a prerequisite for buy-in managers to possess, the option was a strong one to pursue.

The business was being managed by one person, and it was known to be underperforming with problems in meeting customer orders. They had won increased orders from retailers by competing on price, having discounted to below their prices of four years earlier whilst the competition had increased prices by as much as 30 per cent – but they had not predicted the implications of increased demand at lower prices, which caused cash and capacity to be squeezed at tight profit margins.

The opportunity, as understood by the buyers, is represented by the SWOT analysis below.

STRENGTHS	WEAKNESSES
• Established brand and market position. • Cost advantage over market leader. • Retail and distributor relationships. • Stable pattern of demand.	• Poor buyer relationships. • No consumer contact. • No market research. • No marketing. • Brand under exploited. • Lack of product development. • Disorganised – logistics and production failing to match orders.

OPPORTUNITIES	THREATS
• Relatively stable market. • Use of focused and imaginative marketing can yield significant growth. • Improved product design can raise prices and demand. • Relationship marketing direct with consumer can trigger repeat purchases as child grows. • Independent retailers. • Untapped export markets.	• Buyer de-listing. • Reputation for non-delivery. • Long-term decline in birth rate and demand.

David started initial research at the grassroots by visiting stores, talking to retailers and customers and getting a first-hand feel for the business from the market place. He commented:

> *My interest grew because here was an inherently good product but it hadn't been particularly well marketed. It seemed to indicate that there's a business that was profitable, although it needed investment to expand and grow. It had probably reached its peak, given the circumstances it was being run under.*

As the buy-in progressed, the need for greater financial control and production management capabilities, to bring about substantial improvements in these areas of the business, became apparent. Terry, the financial director, joined the management team as its third member at this stage. He also had worked with David previously, and brought both the financial expertise and experience of running a manufacturing facility that the business required.

All three members of the MBI team not only had experience of the toy industry, but they also knew each other and had previous working relationships. A level of trust and mutual respect had developed from those earlier experiences, a situation quite unlike those where a MBI 'team' of complete strangers is brought together. As David described the team:

> *What we bring to this business is a very strong propensity to market successfully. I've got two strong guys alongside me who, have got complementary skills: one very strong on selling and marketing, another very strong on finance.*

The management team, therefore, did not have to learn to work together, rather its members intuitively understood how to do so, in order to turn the business round.

The MBI Process

The professional corporate financial advisors identified potential venture capital investors. An outline strategy and plan were developed to show potential backers what they could do with the business. David commented on the difficulty of developing a business plan based on limited information.

> *We put a plan together prior to coming into the business, which MBI experts tell me is always a stab in the dark because you really are coming in totally blind, despite the assistance from your accountants.*

The team and their backers had to work out an offer price for the business and to put in a bid. The psychology of negotiation played its part at this crucial stage as the buyers were fired-up and keen to buy whilst the vendor clearly aimed to maximise the sale price, as David recalled.

> *There was no price advertised for the business, we worked on multiple sustainable earnings to put our bid in. We put an initial bid in to the vendor, which at that stage could have been rejected by the vendor, and this is where I think a lot of bids fail. There was a process of continued dialogue, and he said, 'You're not bidding enough, you need to up your bid…I'm not going to give you exclusivity on the deal, you're running alongside another agreement, I want to make a decision on this day so you'd better come up with your final offer.' You have to decide is that a game of bluff, because there may not be another bidder. We made our final bid and then got the phone call saying they wanted to finalise it, and we agreed a final figure there and then. From then on we went into due diligence, checked things through and finalised it.*

Conclusions

David's reflections on the acquisition were:

> *I think that I would be a little bit more demanding on the vendor prior to purchase, I'd bang on the table a bit harder. I relied on my financial advisor's advice. Having gone through it, and seen what's here versus what was provided before we bought it, I would have liked more information. I think the other thing is not to underestimate your value, and I don't believe I have, in the transaction and in the whole business set-up, it's all about good management and having people coming to a business who can make it happen.*

At the moment we've just dug into the business, got under the skin of it, ripped it apart and said, this is what we need to do to make it work in the way we think it can work.

He assessed the key qualities he brought to the venture as:

I think a vision of where it can go to and how we need to get there, so a vision and a method of achieving that mission. Strong, tight controls, giving visibility of the business and I would hope the ability to lead and motivate the people that are part of it.

Alistair commented that corporate experience had prepared him by developing the skills and mindset to operate effectively in fast-moving businesses. The challenges they faced could be resolved by systematically applying the approaches that work effectively in larger, more complex businesses. He commented on the acquisition:

When you're in the company, I guess the famous saying is don't expect – inspect, and the hardest thing to do is to try and inspect everything as quickly as possible, without missing things.

From the perspective of having been in senior management roles in large corporations, Terry's analysis was that it was more difficult to bring about change as a buy-in team in an undermanaged business than in a corporate role.

You don't have the detailed knowledge of the way the business runs, so it's a huge learning curve because small businesses tend not to have systems, policies, procedures or high-quality staff – you're learning by experience and I think the thing I've learned is it's taken longer to actually move the business to where we want it to be than I expected it would.

To these reflections can be added the following factors which can contribute to the success of a buy-in.

• An entrepreneurial team, with prior experience of working together, is likely to have enhanced prospects for bringing about successful transformation of the business than a team that is inexperienced in working together or a lone entrepreneur buying a business.

• The buyer must have complete credibility since his track record as a MD, understanding of the sector, ability to invest, personal circumstances and health will be examined minutely.

• Achieving synergy and compatibility between the MBI team, the professional advisors and venture capital investors is essential, with a skilled negotiating team. Most MBI teams will only do it once and are reliant on their professional advisors. Common expectations between the MBI team and the venture capital investor on the speed of the business turnaround, the continuing support needed and the potential for return on investment is important.

- During the acquisition process, accountants and lawyers can see the potential high fee pay-off and may be reluctant for there to be any impediment to complete, especially given the fact that 60 per cent of buy-ins fail and their payment is dependent on completion. The buyer must remember that he is in control, even though the deal seems to acquire a momentum of its own.

- Keeping the options open, having more than one deal available, being objective and in control, and avoiding the risk of the auction-goer's emotional commitment to buying something no matter what, are essential. It may be in the buyer's best interests to delay, withdraw and look for a better deal. Alternatively, being creative in making the deal happen – for example, in closing a gap between the asking and offer price through a staged payment with a second payment dependent on profit performance.

- The buy-in management needs to have experience and capabilities that exceed the challenges they expect to find in the business. There are likely to be a few hidden surprises in any acquisition. In some cases, although not this one, sellers have been known to conceal fundamental problems which have only become evident after acquisition. Whatever the problem, the buyers need to be able to resolve the situation rapidly.

Questions to Consider In Relation to a Management Buy-in

- What are the advantages and disadvantages of a buy-in of an existing business, in comparison with starting a new venture?
- What are the characteristics of an ideal business to acquire?
- What are the characteristics of the ideal entrepreneur to lead a MBI?
- What are the essential steps in completing a MBI successfully?
- What factors could prevent a MBI from being completed successfully, and how could these be predicted or prevented?

CHAPTER 6

Growing the Business

INTRODUCTION

The aim of this chapter is to explore the processes involved in growing a business. This will be achieved through combining a discussion of the key questions related to business growth with the specific experiences of entrepreneurs.

Chapter 5 looked at the process of becoming involved with a venture, whether it be a new or pre-existing business. At that stage, the entrepreneur has become committed: they have 'bought into' the business, not just metaphorically or financially, but for real. Once the decision and the investment have been made, the entrepreneur's role changes, from one that is fundamentally about investment appraisal, to one of releasing the 'hidden value' of the business. The task is of realising – and if possible maximising – the potential value which was identified previously. Whatever choices, decisions or investments have been made, the challenge for the entrepreneur is to deliver.

We have discussed earlier (Chapter 4) about whether all businesses should be expected to grow or to be capable of growth. Different definitions and models of growth – linear and the glass ceilings – were also reviewed, and these concepts are especially relevant to this chapter. The conclusion was that businesses which do not seek to grow may have both limited life and limited impact. There is nothing wrong with lifestyle businesses, but entrepreneurs have – quite literally – no business getting involved with no-growth ventures, unless they have recognised some hidden value which involves shaking them up and transforming them to release it. Growth in the value created by the venture (profit) and the value of the venture itself (what someone else will pay to acquire it) are fundamental to and synonymous with entrepreneurship.

So this chapter is basically about how entrepreneurs go about their core task of creating, increasing and releasing value in the ventures with which they engage. Or, at its simplest, how they manage their businesses and how they make money from them. But this is not a simple process, it is often highly complex and that is why this is the longest chapter in the book. The subject matter is broad, comprising both the start-up and survival of new ventures as well as the turnaround and growth of pre-existing businesses. The businesses in question also vary considerably in terms of their size, not least in the area of sales turnover. Such breadth would be divided into separate chapters were businesses themselves to be the prime subject of this book. But since the focus is on the entrepreneur rather than the business, the diverse nature of experi-

ence found in this chapter enables a greater understanding to be gained
of the processes by which entrepreneurs grow their businesses.

As in Chapter 5, the format starts with a series of initial questions
and discussions, which aim to engage your interest and prompt you to
ask your own questions about this stage of the entrepreneurial process.
The experiences of chosen entrepreneurs are then grouped in a series of
themes, which elicit the highly varied nature of their experiences. The
reader is encouraged to read these with their own questions in mind
and to reflect on the learning points and meanings which can be
derived from these narratives.

It is difficult to disentangle the processes of growing a business from
personal growth and learning. For, unless the entrepreneur has 'done it
all before' (which can be a dangerous assumption), growing the business poses a constant, unpredictable series of challenges, problems, and
new situations – all of which are, potentially, valuable learning experiences. They afford opportunities for learning new skills, strategies,
habits and thinking patterns. This process of learning and changing can
be both disturbing – there is so much to do! – as well as tremendously
stimulating and rewarding. Personal growth and learning comes about
through the process of growing the business. The entrepreneur's role
and skills change in the growth process.

Similarly, if a person is resistant to learning different skills and
changing their approach as the business demands change, they may
find that their own inflexibility constrains or even prevents the business
from growing.

Here are some initial questions about the growth phase of the entrepreneurial process.

- What is the aim of growing the business? What can it lead to?
- How can the business grow? What will cause growth?
- Is there a best strategy to achieve growth?
- Are there recognisable stages that the business will go through?
- What can prevent or slow growth and can these traps be avoided?
- Can the entrepreneur manage growth on their own?

What is the Aim of Growing the Business? What can it Lead to?

Growth is normally necessary for the business to survive beyond the
relatively short-term. But the entrepreneur is likely to be much more
ambitious and to seek the maximum potential growth. Rather than simply aiming to go for a minimal rate of growth, they are concerned with
growing the profitability and the value of the business, not running a
'small business'. However, this does depend, fundamentally, on the

entrepreneur's personal goals and driving forces: what do they aim to achieve and what gives them satisfaction?

These personal factors are likely to influence, if not to determine, the longer term aims of growing the business, and what form of growth will enable that aim to be met. Below are three examples of outcomes from growing a business successfully, over the longer term.

1. Become a leading business in its field, remaining independent and owned by the manager(s) and ultimately their families, or perhaps eventually being bought out by the next generation of managers.
2. The business could be grown to the point where it forms an attractive purchase as a trade sale to another, generally larger firm in the same industry or one which wants to grow by acquisition into that industry.
3. Most ambitiously, the aim could be a market flotation, for example onto the Alternative Investment Market (AIM) for smaller companies in the UK.

There are other successful outcomes as well as variations on those listed above but it is as well to be clear about what the options for the business – and the entrepreneur's eventual exit strategy – might be. Also, it is best to have in mind a fourth outcome: where the business does not succeed in the longer term and either fails or the founder withdraws from it and does something else. Clearly this is not a desirable outcome, but it happens to many people, including some who subsequently go on to become successful entrepreneurs. If the business does fail, it may be that the original decision to enter it was a misjudgement, or that the owner lacked or did not learn sufficiently quickly the capabilities needed to make it successful. Hopefully, they will be able to learn from their mistakes and either do things differently next time or pursue an alternative career.

How can the Business Grow? What will Cause Growth?

Many businesses do grow, at least initially, because the original judgements made about the concept needed were about right and the entrepreneur also does enough things right and with sufficient determination and perseverance to achieve worthwhile results. Alternatively, it is a constant series of struggles – to get started, to find the finance, to win the customers and their orders, to fulfil the orders, to make a profit – but after a while it starts to come right, and then the business establishes an operational pattern which works and the business starts to grow. Neither model sounds very precise or well-organised, but they are fairly typical of the ways in which very many new businesses start.

In order to grow more seriously there are three interrelated things which the business needs to do. The first is to be very clear about what factors will cause or drive growth in its specific marketplace. What is the value that the business is creating or unlocking for its customers? The second is to have a strategy for growth and a plan to grow which is based on this definition of the market and the value created. The third is to be able to put that strategy into operation and to make it work with a combination of total commitment and determination on the one hand, and a sensitivity to changing trends and flexibility to recognise and exploit tactical opportunities on the other hand. And these things can only be done successfully by learning 'what works' for the business and putting it into practice; the development and use of personal theory is fundamental for growth.

Is there a Best Strategy to Achieve Growth?

There are many different strategies and ways in which these can be conceptualised. The growth strategy is highly individual, depending on the aims, the context of the market and situation the business is in and the choices made (see Chapter 4). Rather than there being a 'best strategy', we can see the strategy as a way, perhaps the most important way, in which the entrepreneur's learning and thinking about themselves, the business and the marketplace are used to provide a direction and a plan for the business. In the end, a strategy can only be judged by the results it delivers.

Are there Recognisable Stages that the Business will go through?

Chapter 4 touched on the linear models of growth stages. However, it is questionable how useful these models really are to practising entrepreneurs unless the model can predict, fairly reliably, the steps that should be taken by the business to manage its growth. The 'glass ceilings' model cited does help to do this.

What can Prevent or Slow Growth and How can these Traps be Avoided?

Some of these factors should be apparent by now from preceding chapters. A failure to learn and develop effectively from the market, from technology and from people, including oneself, is one factor, manifesting itself as a lack of management capability in the business. Connected with this, either insufficient resources or poor management of available resources in the following key areas frequently constitutes a barrier to growth.

- **Finance**: working capital, cash.
- **Customers**: finding sufficient profitable buyers.
- **People**: capabilities, expertise, teamwork.
- **Suppliers and distributors**: commitment and capability.
- **Capacity**: premises, technology and equipment.
- **Information**: to enable the best decisions to be made at the right time.

Again, each business will discover its individual limiting factors and barriers to growth. The best way yet discovered of avoiding or reducing the effect of such barriers is to plan – to identify what the constraints are likely to be in achieving your goals, to look at different contingencies (e.g. What do we do if our biggest customer/market is suddenly closed to us?) and to plan what you can do about it. Do it often. Managing a growing business is a holistic process because in growth, every aspect of the business will encounter growth, changes, strains and pressures of different types and at different times. You have to attend to them all and if you can predict what they might be in advance and start to address them before they bite, preferably through delegating responsibility for some of them to other people in the business, it will reduce the need for you to go round sorting out problems in 'fire fighting mode'.

Can the Entrepreneur Manage Growth on their Own?

The myth of the heroic lone entrepreneur is a powerful one, but it is nevertheless largely a myth. Behind every successful entrepreneur and business there is usually an effective team. Sometimes, the business is a 'teamstart', but more commonly a team develops as the business grows, with the two processes being closely interlinked. There are often complex issues here. An entrepreneur may often be highly individualistic, driven and 'not a team player' which can make them difficult to work with or for. If so, this will constrain the growth of the business. No one person *can do* everything, if growth is to be sustained. It is very hard even to *control* everything, which many people also try to do. Either the growth, or the person, will at some stage burn out, which amounts to the same thing. The entrepreneur needs to realise that as the business grows – and for the business to grow – increasingly they will achieve results through other people, not through their own, sole efforts.

There is an interesting process that many MDs of growing businesses seem to follow. They start out as specialists with expertise in a given area, for example, computing, law, finance, sales or engineering. They are skilled in that area and initially that is sufficient. But as the business grows, they realise that they have to develop a rounded, holistic ability to manage the business – including aspects such as finance, marketing, planning, people, and so on – for which their specialist training did not equip them. So they try to manage all aspects of the business, with varying degrees of success. There generally comes a point, sooner or later, when they realise that they need or want to focus their energies more specifically on certain aspects where their capabilities are of most value to the business, such as directing it. They feel they need to 'learn to let go'. At that stage, if they haven't done so before, they try to hire some capable people to run the different parts of the business and they start to build a team. The alternative is, of course, to bring in people with real potential to grow their capability much earlier on, to let them take responsibility as they are ready, and for them to grow and learn with the business.

These questions and responses were intended to stimulate your thinking about what is involved in growing a venture. Before moving to the next section, take a short break to think about the following exercise.

Exercise

What questions do *you* think are the key ones to ask about growing a venture?

The rest of this chapter is divided into a series of themes, each featuring extracts from the stories of people managing growing businesses. The themes reflect some of the most significant issues in the growth process and comprise:

- strategy;
- planning;
- getting close to customers;
- market development;
- product development;
- controlling the business;
- changing the management approach;
- getting results through people.

Finally, there is a study of the turnaround of a business and new product development.

THEMES

Strategy

The strategy for growth, as suggested in Chapter 4, is the direction through which the business will achieve its goals. Strategic thinking is essential if the business is to do more than simply go from one short-term opportunity to another, which will tend to result in the business being constantly in survival mode. Strategy involves having a clear direction and purpose and taking control of the business to achieve the goals.

First, Barry and Linda talk about their growth strategy for the etching business. Faced with fast growth through rapid adoption of their service by customers, together with the success of their customer-friendly approach, their strategy has to be based on the need to respond quickly to changing requirements. Fast growth is hard to control whilst speed in making decisions and taking action is essential.

> *Our view is a company cannot stand still, if it does so it will die. So you have to keep looking to the future, you've got to have a driver, you've got to do it.*

> Barry

> *We started in a recession, which slowed down our cash flow and our growth but made us a bit more streetwise. Now we are in a situation where we have had tremendous growth, two years ago it was 48 per cent, one year ago it was 42 per cent, last year it was 22 per cent, year-on-year, so you are talking about a hell of a growth rate which is quite difficult to control. And we found out our suppliers can't grow as fast as we can. So we had to start our own tool room, we have set up a company next door to do forming, we might even end up doing our own plating because we need the fast turnover. People don't stock anything anymore, and you have got to be able to turn orders around quickly.*

> Linda

This sense of having to grow and doing so organically, by stages – adding on functions, whilst becoming steadily more professional and better all round – is also recounted by Mark as he describes how a move to larger premises enabled his engineering business to grow and to resolve previous problems. However, although he sees turnover doubling, he thinks there is a finite target for the growth of the manufacturing part of his business, and his strategy is rather one of growing a group of businesses around a nucleus.

> *I could have said I'll stop where I am, I've got £1-1¼ million turnover out there, however, you cannot stand still. I could see if we stopped there*

we would just go down the slippery slope and when I was told that years ago I just couldn't understand it but I can now and it would definitely happen. So we have to grow, we have the facilities now. We are going to be efficient, we've shown and demonstrated that, the deliveries have become better, more reliable, the workforce we've got are a lot happier because they are not in a crowded environment and all that coming together now has given us a good leap to the next transition. I would say we could probably do £2½ million now but I wouldn't want it to be much bigger than that.

The future is to have the design facilities as a separate company responsible for its own costs and with its own personal approach to customers, and the manufacturing also separate. I will then latch onto that another couple of companies, whether we start them up ourselves or take somebody over who is struggling, to bring the same management that we have here into those companies. So each module will be operating in its own right with its own customers. I feel that if we get too big or too remote then we start to lose that personal touch and the continual contact and communication with the customer.

Mark

Anna's computer services business achieved spectacular growth in its early years even though it is in an industry where high growth rates are common. But the reasons she cites for that growth show a very clear perception of where the value added by the business is coming from, in line with the move from being product to service focused.

I think within the first twelve months we went from two people to fifteen people and within three years we were up to 40 people turning over £4 million so we were a successful company straight away. I attribute that to technology that was changing, the people I had on board were so eager to learn with the technology, and they believed in what they were doing. I believe it was the enthusiasm of all the staff and myself who were very highly motivated by it all that made the company immediately successful.

We are now very much a service-orientated company. We used to sell purely boxes and hardware and make lots of money out of it, but now it is very much a commodity product, and we had to learn through experience, through the fact that we can't make £3,000 on a computer anymore, we're lucky if we make £30, because the margins have eroded. So we have to go out and look for where the money is, how can we maximise the profit of these deals. We do this through selling our people, selling our skills, and we train our people quite heavily in the products and the services so that they can deliver the customers a better service that they don't mind paying for.

Anna

The three enterprises described so far are relatively young businesses whose strategies reflect a very clear commitment to growth, where the whole culture is very much growth oriented. That entrepreneurial, customer-focused, fast-moving and energetic culture has been moulded very much by the entrepreneurs who founded and still run the businesses. Those we now look at reflect more complex situations in longer established businesses. The next example is given by Brian, describing how his ambitious growth strategy to take advantage of the opportunities to go for very fast growth in the tool hire industry were not supported by his co-directors, and the opportunity was lost.

> *I failed to persuade my partners on the way we should expand. They said we're successful here, we should expand little by little and consolidate which made us a very strong company, we had so many branches in this city and we have always been by far the strongest here. But as I advocated at the time, once we could see it was working here, my strategy was to be big and to push right out to Birmingham and London and to fill in later. We would have been very big today had we done so.*

Brian

This account shows clearly the emergence of different aims for the business, bringing a highly entrepreneurial agenda which identified and aimed to exploit a window of opportunity for rapid growth into conflict with more cautious aims for steady, organic growth. The next, extended account is the continuation of John's story of how he brought about strategic change in the retail business he ran. It illustrates the complexity of developing and implementing an ambitious growth strategy in a business that was still family-owned. The theme of needing to have the right strategy at the right time in relation to the market situation is should to be essential. It also shows the need for regular renewal within the business to bring in fresh, innovative capability.

> *One of my favourite theories of business is that of the cycle, all businesses go through a cycle, and after a while lethargy sets in: you know it all, you've done it all before, you have got to be right and that leads to deterioration and at that stage a good entrepreneur has to identify that and has to do something about it. At the time, the company was having all sorts of problems with its shareholders. We were in the middle of an expansion programme and I realised that the merchandiser was beginning to slow down. I left him alone and concentrated on the bigger problem of the family ownership. When I got back to concentrate on the business, I did change the management, but we were three years late in doing it. I didn't have much time and I wanted to be in at the beginning of the consolidation that was going to take place in the industry rather*

than at the end because one of the strategic problems we had was to move the business out of town.

So the company was going through a very dramatic structural change, moving very fast out of town at the same time as trying to change the management. I felt that, whilst those changes were going through very well, the merchandising was not keeping up and in retailing merchandising is everything. So I decided it was not working, what will we do, who is the best retailer? I identified the best retailer but, unfortunately, he would not move so we effectively bought his company.

That company was bigger than ours, so we merged the companies which had all sorts of wonderful effects, one we got their very young and talented management, two, we got quantum, three, it gave me the opportunity to get rid of the family once and for all, and four, it gave me the opportunity that once we had rationalised the two businesses and done the next acquisition, I could become a non-executive director and get on with my life. So that was looking at the issues from the purely strategic point of view, and again identify the problem, identify the solution and have the determination to ram it through against everybody; the family, the shareholders, the directors didn't want to do it. The only person who wanted to do it was me and I was right. They didn't want to do it for all the wrong reasons, the emotional, security reasons, all those things. It is fair to say that I carried them with me by dragging them through the hedge backwards, it was really 'follow me men, you will follow me otherwise I will leave you behind'.

The result was that the company was yet again reinvigorated, for the third time in fact, and we went on to do the next acquisition. I did what I think was the best deal for the company. Now the business is certainly most successful and amongst the biggest in the sector. I think we are certain to grow as we have the best management, young, dynamic, entrepreneurial, all those things, the best management team that I have ever seen.

John

The personal dynamism and determination required to force change through the business is highly evident here. Having realised that introducing major changes sequentially was too slow in relation to changes in the retail industry, John saw the need to avoid stagnation and was able to combine the strategies of moving out of town, growing by acquisition and, by a reverse takeover, re-energising the business and changing the shareholding structure. In doing this, he also created his own route for moving out of running the business, which we shall return to in the next chapter. To be able to formulate and push through a strategy, with which others may well disagree and oppose, the entrepreneur must have a clear mental picture of what they want to achieve, combined with complete belief that they will achieve it and determination to do so, no matter what. David's reflection about the business turnaround following the MBI described at the end of Chapter 5 encapsulates this.

> *One of my favourite poems is 'If' by Kipling, I think it's a wonderful poem and I read it from time to time. You've just got to have a belief that this is the way that its going to be done, that this is the vision we've got and I'm sure it will work, provided we all work to these factors – believe me it can be done. And I know it can be done and we will get there.*
>
> David

Planning

The growth strategy is very much concerned with the direction of the business in relation to the market environment. Planning is a much more specific, detailed process of deciding priorities, actions and allocating resources. Here Anna describes how the planning process works in her business, through assimilating information from industry leaders to develop a plan based around their product portfolio.

> *We plan by always reading ahead, the Internet is a great font of knowledge, we use it an awful lot to look at what other companies are doing. We work very closely with some of the large players. We plan but we are market led, we get to know what Microsoft and Compaq are doing, we look at their strategies and we try and match them with ours to see if it fits into our portfolio of products. We then take that campaign and productise it so that we can give it to our sales force to go out and sell.*
>
> Anna

The 'we' in Anna's account suggests planning is an inclusive process. This is more explicit in the next account from Linda, as she describes how the directors now engage the management team and through them everyone in the business in a holistic planning process.

> *We have been more proactive in bringing managers in on planning than we had been, before it was something that we, as principals, had just done. Our starting point is always the operational budget, what did we do last year, look at the accounts, see how we are going to grow, anticipate from the movement in the accounts, the feel from sales, how the market is going to go, what kind of growth we can expect and then feed that into an operational budget. We look at what kind of net profit we are going to get and what we're going to invest to help us meet that turnover.*

Each manager goes to their department and they have a departmental meeting. If we think we're going to get 28 per cent growth, what does your department need to meet that? They talk to everybody and put together a wish list, they do a versatility chart of people and their skills. They bring all that information plus a report of what they completed last year to a planning meeting. Then we look at where the growth is going to be, for example is it in formed parts: What extra training do we need? What extra personnel? What extra equipment? Finally we overlay all the main goals and look at every aspect of the business for the overall view to ensure it all matches up.

Linda

In this way the planning process is used to do a complete assessment of the capability of each part of the business to meet expected requirements and grow in relation to the overall projections for sales and profits. Even in a fast-growing business, last year's performance is still regarded as a powerful predictor for the future.

The next three themes look at three distinct strategies for growth which arise from the Ansoff matrix (see Chapter 3): developing existing markets through getting close to customers, developing new markets and developing new products.

Getting Close to Customers

This strategic option is based on gaining a very detailed understanding of the size, the potential, the spending habits and preferences of market sectors where the business already trades, focusing on current customers. The first account is from Alistair, who describes his approach to researching the child safety-seat market, into which his company is selling, starting with the competitive positions of the different suppliers and re-sellers. The business had previously not carried out any market research nor had direct contact with the purchasers of its products, so direct consumer research was used to find out about them.

The key things that I needed to know were, first of all, what's the total size of the industry? What are the sterling shares in the market? Who's growing? Who's falling? What are the sectors? What's the value of those sectors? Which sectors are increasing or decreasing? Then what's the sterling share? What's the unit share? What are the retailers' shares? The individual sectors? Who's growing? What's the share that our customers have within those sectors?

But you can't beat actually talking to the consumer. The next piece of work we did was actually getting to the consumer and running some hard qualitative research. We decided to do what we believed to be the largest ever consumer research project within the industry. We now know what the consumer thinks about the industry, and, together with the market research, we could then really start to say that we understand enough of where the market is, what the opportunities are, who's doing what, what the consumer wants, how are we now going to tell the consumer about our great product developments. And really, new product development is the life and blood of any company and, because there was a complete lack of innovation within the business, what we were looking to do was to make some immediate changes to get to the consumer very fast so they can start to have confidence, but also look at new product development further down the street.

Alistair

Gathering and analysing thorough, up to date and reliable information about the market is clearly of essential importance here, leading to informed decisions about market opportunities, improving communications with customers, upgrading existing products, and new product development. Using customer information effectively is crucial, as Linda describes.

We've got a service which is an excellent thing in times of recession because what we do is re-focus where we're targeting our marketing, now we have got customers from fashion, aerospace, automotive, electronics industry, jukeboxes and when we find that our customers who are in one sector such as telecommunications are having setbacks, we have to re-focus.

It's building on that relationship with our customers who cover a wide spectrum of industries so that we can pick up the information, the little signs. It's backed up with our customer database, so we can pull out a section and say, 'What was a particular customer doing for us last year? What are they doing this year, we ought to go out and see them — is somebody else getting our work or is there just something going on in their industry?' Also I look at the actual size of the accounts, the regularity of payments, that is crucial. So our first port of call for our information of what is happening out there is our customers.

Linda

In the next account, Mark describes his use of retained information within the business about existing customers and how he has developed the relationships with these customers to find out about their problems and to position his business to add much more value by giving them a solution. In this way, he has progressed from simply being a subcontractor to a much closer and more rewarding relationship.

My strategy is now I have a database of turnovers with different companies, I know the margins that we make, each job is given a unique number so we know what job we've made money on. I've taken the view that it's cheaper and easier to keep and develop the customers you've got than have the expense of going out to find new ones, I think the figures are that it costs you 60 per cent more to find a new customer than it does to keep an existing one.

I have always wanted to do design work because I saw that people did not want to go out to various different companies and what better than to have a fabricator that does design as well because he is going to design it such that it's going to be made economically and easily. It's primarily the personal contact with them, the ability to be able to talk to them, not just get a drawing and a quotation but to discuss it with them, continual communication with them and assistance as well. We find that, once you are in at that level, they have got so much confidence in you and you build up a rapport with them they very rarely go to anyone else.

In a lot of businesses that we deal with, the people are under so much pressure because of restructuring and redundancies, they just can't do everything and haven't got the time to think. So that's where we come in, because we're helping them with a solution when they're just bogged down, fed up with 12-13 hours a day and they see us as a good way of resolving those problems without their resources, so we say we'll come in, we'll measure up, we'll price it up, if we get the job we'll then come back in and we'll get our fabricators to do it.

Mark

This strategic path involves learning about, learning from and learning (to solve problems) with customers. It creates mutual value: a win-win equation where the business' unique understanding of the customers' needs and the strength of the relationship create new opportunities and encourage customer spending to increase and higher margins to be earned, since the importance of price alone within the buying equation will tend to decrease.

Market Development

Market development involves targeting a market new to the business which offers opportunities for supplying existing products and services. It is often necessary for new ventures, if they do not start in a sector with which they are familiar. Where there is limited growth potential in familiar markets, market development becomes essential. It does require sophisticated marketing and selling skills to avoid the trap of wasting resources. It means learning about and from the market; since what is effective in one market will not automatically transfer to another and effective research is essential, as is knowing what capability and value you are bringing to the market.

Brian's description shows how his business applied the formula which worked well in tool hire to the catering hire market, and took advantage of a timely opportunity to enter this market. The catering operation went on to be highly successful.

> *We realised that you could apply the principle of hire to other things and we always thought catering hire would be a good thing to do. We had an extremely successful branch in a very good location, and then we moved our central hire depot to nearby which took the business away from this branch. But we did not want to close it and my colleague said, 'I think it is our moment to try catering.' Now we knew we wanted to do this and a challenging situation came along which gave us the opportunity to try. I believe catering became immediately successful because we chose the right moment and because a set of circumstances arose and we made the best use of them. So timing is everything, you get some wrong and you get some right but of course you hope that you get most right.*
>
> Brian

Next, Mark describes his approach to targeting and opening up clients in new sectors for his engineering business. His approach to the pharmaceutical sector is highly focused and he is very clear about the result he intends to achieve.

> *I quickly identified that I wanted to work for blue-chip companies. I was getting a lot of business by reading* The Daily Telegraph, *looking in the appointments page at companies that were taking on project managers, so a letter and a brochure went out. We started to get a fair hit rate from reading the trade press, pharmaceuticals and water were up and coming so they were the areas I started to target. The food industry also, because in the early days the idea was to be a specialist in stainless steel, very few people were about in stainless steel at the time. So my niche markets were anybody who wanted anything made out of stainless steel.*
>
> *I am putting an advert in the* Pharmaceutical Journal *because all the customers I deal with read it, and that will be money well spent because there's nobody advertising in there for designing and manufacturing. I am doing a specific mail shot to those pharmaceutical companies that I want to deal with. I purchased a mailing list, I will look at the type of work that we're doing at the moment, look at the type of work we're good at and we're making good margins on and try and get the mail shot arranged around that type of business and then follow up again to make sure they've received it. I will go in, give them a presentation to probably 25 companies. So keeping it relatively small but the quality will be there.*
>
> Mark

In any market, be it an existing or a new one, being different and innovative to engage the customer's attention is always important.

The key to marketing I always say is if you've got the creativity and innovation, yet as long as you stay one step ahead of your competitors, you'll never be beaten. Now the challenge is to come up with new ideas that are bigger and better, but won't necessarily cost any more money.

Alistair

Product Development, Innovation, Adding Value

Here the opportunity is to develop new products and services for existing markets in which there are opportunities for growth. Innovations and extra value-added services can be offered to gain additional income from known markets. It involves using knowledge about known markets and combining this with innovating new products and processes. It is important to be customer-led in developing new products for which there is real demand (or where demand can be stimulated) and, therefore, to be aware of market trends. It is also an opportunity to unlock the underused value in existing knowledge, capability or capacity, such as in other people's products which can be offered into markets which you understand.

Here, Anna describes how her business matches new IT products to the market segments it knows well, using the example of the legal market. The process here involves learning about the new product and *'commoditising it'* so that repeat sales can be made more easily.

We identify projects and go and vertically sell. We don't take every opportunity, we take the opportunities that we can capitalise on and work with, then we go out there and sell and know that we can do it well. We try and match our skills to what our customers want and then we can deliver them a better service. So it is very much matching our skills with our vertical market areas, we match the products with our customers and then try and sell it. We always look at a product and say if it fits that solicitor then it should fit every solicitor, because they may work slightly different but they all have the same goals. We'll try and match to each solicitor and do repetitive selling, so we commoditise it and it becomes less of a pain for us every time we do it. The first one is always difficult and then after that it becomes a commodity.

Anna

New product development can also provide the opportunity to achieve greater efficiency by squeezing extra value from a process that is not performing at peak efficiency. This is demonstrated by the example of a leather manufacturer of fashion apparel. The firm was losing money and was a seasonal business in which sufficient hides were bought in six months to resource twelve months production, which did not help cash flow. There were high rates of wastage in addition to higher costs from producing leather to meet the best standard. By changing the production process and creating a new market for an embossed finish leather which could use the lower-grade raw material, wastage was cut and output quality improved from 50 to 97 per cent. Together with other economies, the business moved into profit within two years.

Earlier in this section, Mark described how in his engineering business he was able to sell higher value services into existing customers through relationship development. Here he describes how he used his knowledge of the water industry combined with the design and fabrication capabilities of his business to go to the next stage of introducing his own products as a strategic move which provided the business with a unique product and lessened its dependence on subcontracting.

> *We have developed one or two of our own products as another strategic move. We do access covers for the water industry, which are now trademarked, I've taken on an ex-Anglian Water guy to sell those and that's worked really well. That took six or seven years to get established. Now what I need is other products to follow that; I am constantly thinking what it will be or where it will come from. I quickly learnt that you couldn't just rely on subcontract work in engineering; if I was totally reliant on subcontract work I would have been long gone.*

> Mark

Finally, we look at the strategy of reducing risk by being a 'market follower' rather than an innovator in the context of John's retail business. Given that failed innovation can be extremely expensive – just as successful innovation can be highly profitable – this is a lower risk, lower return route.

> *We were never the innovators, we were always the followers. I always believed in eliminating a lot of the risk in terms of marketing because I was never a natural merchant so I was always very careful to watch the trends. When I saw a trend that I believed in and could strategically back up, we would look at the figures and build on that rather than rely purely on a gut feeling. Then we would move fast because we always had good people, who worked very hard, so when we decided to do something we did it very quickly and caught up.*

> *The true entrepreneur made the judgement and got it right, the poor entrepreneur got it completely wrong, and people like me who were opportunistic saw what had happened, watched it and then came in one stage later. But I think coming in one stage later is much safer than coming in at the beginning.*

> John

This strategy is only made possible by compressing development and implementation times in the way described. Given the phenomenon in almost all industries of a very rapid progression from innovation, to replication by followers, to commoditisation, the issue of speed and timing of response – being able to enter the market before everyone else does too – is a critical one. Just as for the innovators is the need to keep innovating, and to do so in hard-to-replicate ways, since the followers will very quickly copy successful innovations.

Controlling the Business

As the business grows, it is essential to have firm and effective controls over the key processes. Monitoring sales and controlling costs and cash flow is, of course, vital in any business. An effective control system, and the information it generates, enables key indicators and trends to be followed and acted on. Whilst each entrepreneur might have individual ways of doing this, the fundamentals remain very much the same. We saw in Chapter 5 how Mike, in the story of his new business, had built it around control systems. Here Terry describes the problems inherent in taking over a business without adequate financial information, in this case the child car-seat business. He sees the priority as being to lower fixed costs and to be the lowest cost supplier in the industry.

> *One of the key things in a business, particularly in a business you haven't been in before, is knowing what the trends are, and we miss good numbers. You control the business by the numbers. Experience tells us that when you're working in a volatile marketplace, where your volume can go up and down, the lower you can get your fixed costs, the more secure the business is. So we have a view that anywhere we can lower our fixed costs, and make them variable, without compromising quality, customer service or costs, we should do that. I have a very firm belief that you have to be the lowest cost supplier because, if you're not, then you will be unable to invest the maximum amount of money in marketing, sales activity, building the brand, and it's really those areas that are going to secure the long-term prosperity of the company.*
>
> Terry

Another book in this series will give a detailed treatment of the financial management issues, so they will not be expanded on here.[1] However, to show how a widespread (and often criticised) management system can be used to provide operational control of a business, here is Mark's description of how the quality management system works in his business to provide visibility of key processes.

---

1. Marshall *Dynamic Financial Management* (Blackhall Publishing, October 1999).

The ISO 9002 quality management system helps us run the business because starting off as a small company you have got various tasks to do, so it formalised the structure and it got us into a routine where you do the essential things, like recording the quotations, so that you know what enquiry levels you've got coming in, how many you are converting, and when you get orders you record them, you set up a file for it and you follow it all the way through.

Mark

Managing the Business

The entrepreneur, by definition, is personally committed to the business and its success. This is necessary to achieve success but taken too far and for too long, there is a danger that it becomes obsessive and impossible to walk away from. At some stage, it is necessary to realise that they are managing the business, as opposed to being the business. 'Learning to let go' is a general 'growing pain' for entrepreneurs. Here Anna describes how she worked through this experience.

I was wanting to work till 11-11.30 at night which has a detrimental effect on your family and I think the pressures make you think, 'Hold on, you could lose everything here.' I wasn't happy because I was being pulled everywhere, so I had to make time slots, going back to setting goals again, saying, 'I will work till 7.00 at night and then I finish and when I go home it's family time, weekends are family time.' And I actually ended up having to set myself goals.

I realised after about six months when I had let people get on with it that it was very hard for me to step back in. I started working on one very big deal, we got the order and it was great and then I left that to go onto something else whilst everybody else sorted it out. That's really how we grew the company, and we appointed some very good managers to look after it. But that was quite difficult because it meant letting go and that is where for anybody who started off and has been very involved as the focal point, letting go of the reins is the hardest thing. That is really how we did grow, because I was the force who had hold of these reins actually let them go and let everyone get on with it. It has allowed me to concentrate and to have the free time to go and do some of my own things now.

Anna

Mark, similarly realised that in working all-out to meet customer requirements he had become overreactive to customers and was not focused enough on running his business profitably. Again, he describes how he worked to get back in control through making clear decisions and being selective about orders and customers, and starting to delegate.

*Three years ago – the business was running me, my customers were run-
ning me, and it made me look at the hard facts and look at the figures and
think, 'Why on earth have I been doing that for so long? I'm not having it
anymore, I am going to start running a business and I am going to start
running my customers and if I think they're wrong then I'm going to tell
them they're wrong.' And it's surprising the results you get.*

*We tended to find every so many months we would have a bad patch
and everything would go wrong, we were making no money and the
problem jobs are always those ones where we've had the cheap price,
always those customers that are not willing to pay, and I think it was a
conscious decision then, so I said right I'm going to wheedle these out
and after that I don't care, this is what I'm going to do and I did it.*

*I mean it's only over the last couple of years where I have been in the
position where I can actually say, 'Yes, I am the managing director, I am
now within reason steering this ship.' But it took a long while and that
again was through me not being able to delegate properly and trying to
override different decisions but as I say I'm still hands-on, I'm still close
to what's going on and I always will be.*

Mark

Each entrepreneur will tend to develop their own 'management style'
which they find effective for themselves and for the business. Again,
this is an outcome of their learning about themselves and of how they
achieve results most effectively, and increasingly through other people.
Here John describes his approach: one of listening to all points of view
but then making a firm decision which he implements with total commitment.

*I don't believe there is a right way or a wrong way to run a business,
whether it's top down or bottom up, command and control or consensus. I
think all that matters is the way that suits that particular organisation and
the people in it. What suits me is the ability to discuss and the ability for
people to talk to me and give me their views and I will listen to them and
take them in but when I have made my mind up I am absolutely determined to see it through and that they will do it and they have to be on
board. That's where you get the ruthlessness and the determination.*

John

Anna's description of how her decision making style has changed to be
more open to other peoples' points of view, also shows that she recognised that listening to others and accepting differing approaches was
important.

*I used to be very quick to criticise because I always thought I could do it
better. I would say that has been my biggest learning point because I*

have been in situations where two or three people have done something differently but they have all been right and I wouldn't have done it any of their ways. I used to be quite bullish in doing it my way because I thought my way is right and I know I'm right but I am not necessarily right, so now I can stand back. That comes from listening to other people and taking on board other views.

Anna

One perspective on managing the growing business is that it constitutes a continuous series of problems, challenges and questions which somehow the entrepreneur has to learn to solve. Brian's philosophy, stated here, is one in which the entrepreneur must *'meet the challenges'*, should continually be thinking their way through the challenges, and always be able to give a clear explanation of where they are going, what they are doing, and how and why they are doing it.

In my view you treat every setback as a challenge – how am I going to get round this, get over it, get through it, how am I going to do it? Whatever happens, you never let your head go down and you keep smiling, however bad things are you do what has to be done and you think, 'What is the way round this problem? What is the way over it? How am I going to do it?'; always that question 'How am I going to do it?' and you never ever give in, never. The entrepreneur has to meet these challenges, certainly has to know where he or she is going.

Brian

These last three quotations make clear the entrepreneur's responsibility for making and implementing firm decisions, providing a clear direction and leadership. However, as the business grows there is an increasing dependence on achieving results through others rather than directly by oneself.

People – Getting, Developing and Managing

As the business grows, so the role of entrepreneur – often as MD – shifts increasingly to one of managing people, in which the challenges are those of finding, hiring, motivating, developing and retaining the best people. Alongside this, there is a process of getting better performance from, changing and, if necessary, getting rid of unsatisfactory people. As the nature of growing businesses is increasingly knowledge-based, the importance of these processes is heightened. Just as the entrepreneurial process is one of unlocking value, so managing people can be viewed as one of *'unlocking the value within individuals and teams'*.

In this way, since all people do have inherent capabilities and potential, the entrepreneur's role is at its most productive one of recognising and enabling them to fulfil their potential. This might seem unlikely: how and why should such driven, even self-centred creatures as entrepreneurs do such a thing? In which case, the views of entrepreneurs who have built successful businesses may be rather surprising. Their ability to manage people is fundamental to achieving successful growth of the business to the 'visionary' level in the 'glass ceilings' model (see Chapter 4). Anna describes her approach to training people.

> *People want to learn, people want to better themselves all the time. Within our industry, you have to have a certain accreditation in order to get on and be valued, and an individual who has got that accreditation is worth £10,000 more than an individual who hasn't. As a company, we have always accredited people to the highest level. So it's a continual process, but if we didn't do that we would lose staff anyway and once they have got that accreditation we can sell our staff out for a lot more because they are worth it, and the customer perceives that they are getting good value for money.*
>
> Anna

Anna's business is in the highly competitive IT services industry, where skilled, accredited staff can command high salaries and are notoriously mobile. Even so, it makes commercial sense to train them. What is not conveyed by her quotation is the sense of 'buzz' and energy, which one feels immediately on entering her business, the culture is one of achieving, competing, yet friendly and informal.

A business, which has also evolved a very distinctive culture, is the etching business run by Linda and Barry. Here, the culture is much more one of a large, extended family. Everyone belongs and has a strong sense of shared commitment to making the business a success. Everyone is encouraged to participate in training and development. However, the business was shaken deeply by the untimely death of Linda's husband a few years ago. This forced a fundamental re-think of the way they managed the business and the decision to develop a management team.

> *We decided that no single person or two people being out of the picture must ever jeopardise the security and future of this company. So we decided that we had managers, but we really had to focus on this as a management team, they were all very good at their jobs and their particular skills, whether it was managing sales, production, things like that, but did they work effectively as a team, did they communicate as a team and did they communicate horizontally and vertically? So we decided we needed to identify the areas of weakness and build those up.*
>
> *We are heavily into multi-skilling because we do not like people being bored. What started off as an unskilled function in most companies we have made semi-skilled and, through the commitment of our staff, they*

*have turned it into a skilled function. I would say every one of those
roles out there is highly skilled. They have done that themselves in ten
years and we are very proud of them.*

Linda

Both of these businesses were 'greenfield' and developed their own culture, one which the founders have moulded. That is a quite different
situation from the long-established business, with a deep-rooted culture
that is one of the factors contributing to the underperformance of the
firm. The people issues in turnarounds often require great leadership
and skill to resolve, in which the entrepreneur's role is one of catalyst in
changing the established and suboptimal practices, as David and Terry
indicate in their assessment of the business they took over.

*The people were very demotivated when we joined because of a very
autocratic and unforgiving, non-rewarding management style. The con-
sequence of that is good people won't stay, they'll disappear and you end
up with people who are just followers, and you never get a lot of input
from them. We're still looking for more ideas from our key staff, we're
not getting it from some and I think some of those have to change. We
will gradually improve the quality of the people here but we're keeping it
very lean. We want people who can understand us, work with us and
work at a speed that we believe is right for the business, who can move
us forward and see the vision.*

David

*A small company can be successful to a level, but it probably runs out of
expertise to actually understand how to maintain its growth, or even
maintain its sales volume and that's really where we're trying to take it,
to that next level. But the people have to try to lift their game, and we
have to get the right level of people who can grow the business with us.*

Terry

The next account shows the importance that one very successful MD
attaches to managing people. In particular, note the ways in which he has
handled these critical issues: selection, by hiring smart people, investing
responsibility in people, coaching people to work through problems,
which they think are beyond their capability, and having high expectations of their performance.

*I have always been able to pick people with whom I have been able to work
and develop. I have been extremely proud of the way in which I have developed the people that work for me. You are looking for personality and skill
– people have got to have a good brain, they have got to have a lively intelligence, and a good personality, and they also have to have ambition.*

I say to people, you can do whatever you want, you can take as much responsibility as you want, there is only one criterion: if you are the least bit worried that you can't do it or you have got it wrong, you must tell me because if you tell me I will absolve you of all responsibility and I will deal with it. If you don't tell me, and you get it wrong, you're finished, but if you tell me what the problem is, I will deal with it. The way I deal with it is to explain it and go through it with them, so it is not just 'OK I will see to it', it's 'OK I will see to it, this is the problem, this is how we are going to analyse it, this is what we are going to do about it, now you either do it yourself or I'll do it for you'. What I find is, if you have gone through it thoroughly with somebody, you're working it out for yourself as well as for them, and you agree between you what you should be doing. So they have the benefit of seeing the process and the analysis and having comfort from the fact that I didn't instantly know what the solution was, I had to work it out. They then have the confidence in that judgement and they get up and do it and get the satisfaction from doing it themselves. I find that way you build people's self-confidence and their willingness to come to you.

I've always tried to say, 'What I want you to achieve is this, you go do it and come back when you've done it.' You give them the credit when they have achieved it, and then when they come back and say 'I've done it', I say 'I never thought you would', so they get the ownership, they get the accolade, they get the praise, but I get the benefit and that is really what I am after. It is building up the people around you to make them feel that they are actually better than they are, because if they were as good as they think they are, they wouldn't have needed me to tell them, but in fact they do need me to tell them. I would like to think that I push people to achieve more than they really can achieve by giving them the direction.

John

There are two further significant points in this account. One is that the problem-solving process which John describes using as a coaching tool is exactly the same thinking process as he applied throughout his career; by modelling it in this way he is enabling others to adopt it. The other is that he recognises that his employees need to feel they have achieved the results and the credit that he pushed them to achieve; he is content that the business receives the benefit of their performance.

REVIEW

Go back to the questions you wanted to ask about growing the business. Having read and thought about the themes and the entrepreneurs' stories, what conclusions do you now draw in relation to these questions?

UNLOCKING VALUE
The Story of the Turnaround of an Underperforming Business, Market and New Product Development

The final section of this chapter describes an entrepreneurial approach to turning around an existing business. It draws together many of the themes of this chapter, and demonstrates how these are closely integrated in the growth process. The key areas are those of identifying the growth potential of the business, developing a strategic plan for growth, implementing the strategy successfully, developing new markets and new products, the use of key management controls and, throughout, the process of selecting, managing and developing people.

The narrator is Robert, who started his career as a chemist, then moved into technical services, was trained in work and method study, and developed an ability to pinpoint the causes of underperformance in factories. He moved into the soft drinks, and then into the food industry, gaining experience in poultry, confectionery and commodity products. He is now managing director of a snack foods company. The consistent themes in his career are listed below.

- Developing the capability to turnaround loss-making or underperforming businesses. Simple yet fundamental management tools are used to achieve significant, even transformational results.
- Thinking creatively and laterally to solve problems and create new opportunities.
- Determining clear goals for himself and for the businesses he manages, and then being unshakeably persistent achieving those goals yet highly flexible in the strategies he adopts to do so.
- From an early stage, realising that results came about through others, and that if a business was underperforming then that was because the people in it were being held back.
- Having the determination to realise the maximum profit potential from a venture, and to breakthrough whatever constraints are holding a business back, and then to maximise the value of the business.

Below he describes his first experience as a managing director.

I went in as MD of a confectionery business that had been run down. The management style was fear, and it was a shambolic mess – they didn't know the size of the marketplace, they didn't know the potential sales universe, they hadn't contemplated seriously the export market, they hadn't realised that major multiple grocers were pretty important and they had no serious penetration to that sector. I decided we needed to completely restructure the business from top to bottom.

I set about looking for a new senior team of managers, who I recruited from blue-chip organisations. These were aspiring people, in their upper-20s, who hadn't quite made it yet, who had real spark about them, desperate to prove a point. I had this very keen group of aspiring indi- viduals with points to prove. So I didn't create the position of production director or sales director or marketing director, I let them aspire to that position.

Planning Growth

I sat down and produced what I thought was a sensible 3-year business plan, focusing on markets globally, technical issues, production, etc. and I presented it to the management teams and said, 'The purpose of this pre- sentation is to tear the plan to bits – throw it out, tell me I'm wrong, tell me what it should say!'

I just used it to get people thinking. They didn't tear it apart, we organised a series of six weekly meetings, in which I said, 'I want to have a strategy here, a business plan for years one, two and three that everybody buys into – everybody.' We achieved that in six weeks, and I suppose 70-80 per cent of what I'd written at the beginning was retained at the end.

I started by saying, 'Lets define the sales universe, and I don't mean the accounts that we service today, what's the sales universe, lets not limit our thinking by saying we're a £11 million turnover company now, and so lets do a budget to make ourselves £12 million next year – don't think like that, tell me what the sales universe is!'

We defined a matrix that said, 'Here's the sales universe.' It included America, the Middle East and the Far East, and I said, 'Now tell me what our products are and which of these products are appropriate to those elements of the sales universe; what's the route to market and how do we get it there? Let's not limit ourselves to 10 per cent growth in budget terms!'

*I think that budgets can be incredibly limiting to managers. Why limit ourselves with a budget? If you get the right people, with the right mentality, it's the managing director's job then and each of the budget holders' jobs, to control the cost to an **optimum**, not to a **minimum**, its about **value**, not cost – control those costs to an optimum and then it's about driving your sales to the maximum the business infrastructure can stand, and doing it on a very profitable basis.*

So, with this database of products and sales universe we said, 'Why aren't we selling our products in the major multiple grocers? Let's get on and do it.' We brought in our national account manager and said, 'Your job is to get our products into these accounts' and we got penetration in all the major grocers, except one. There was a big private label base, and we were good at making toffee, so we decided to sell toffee to private labels. We knew we were up against the market leader, so we had to be the lowest cost producer. We got some help to establish the relative cost position, which we would need to be genuinely, the lowest cost producer of a toffee product in the whole world. We recognised we had a very exportable product here, so we established who had the lowest cost and who had the second lowest cost on a worldwide basis and we put a programme together to undermine that and become the lowest cost producer in the world, and we achieved it.

Then we started to export via an agent in America, and we promoted the product and got international distribution throughout the States. We did the same in Holland, the same in the Middle East, where each country had a different trading philosophy and we learnt what that trading philosophy was by visiting the country.

That's something else I learned from this company – if you're going to export, you don't sit at a desk and export, you go to the country, you meet the potential customers, you sit in front of the buyers of these big organisations, because they are not the same as over here. They are different, they have different criteria, and you have to go out and learn it for yourself.

Developing people

One of the most important things for a MD to achieve is to develop his people; it's about never taking anything at face value, coupled with the lesson that says that you can only achieve if you've got the right people.

If there is an individual who's not capable, you don't live with it. As tough as it may be, you take that individual out. You've got to have the right people in your organisation, you can't tolerate weak links so you change the person, get the person in place and then you build that person up.

People are multi-talented and you shouldn't put them in little boxes and say this person is in that box, they're a marketer and that's all they know, and this person is a salesman and that's all they know, and this person is in manufacturing and that's all they know. I took the guy I'd brought in as national account manager, and eventually moved him up to sales director and he did a reasonable job but just as he thought he was getting his feet under the table, I changed his job. I made him manufacturing director, he said he didn't know anything about it and I said I'd help him. He did an even better job as manufacturing director after that than as sales director and he was staggered. He's now moved on, and his forte is now manufacturing rather than sales, he's become rounded and that was a real lesson, it was a real joy to see that.

If there is something good to be achieved and it's a benchmark on the way to success. You don't walk into a room and say, 'Aren't I fantastic, I've just done this?' You engineer it so they walk into the room and say, 'Aren't I fantastic, I've done this?' To which you reply, 'Yes, well done!' So, if there is something that has to be done, and it has not been thought of, you set that seed in somebody's mind and you let them do it and let *them have the success because they are the people you have to coach – you don't dictate, you coach and you let them score the goals.*

Controlling the business

I want a traffic light report in every business I walk into, for every single product that we make. I want to understand the material cost, the direct labour cost, the prime margin and beyond that I want all the variable costs, which include things like the variable distribution cost, so I've got a contribution to all the business' fixed overheads. Then I know what the fixed overheads are, I know what contribution I've got to make and I can make marginal costing decisions based on that.

If you walk into a business off the street and it's losing money how do you turn it round? It's dead easy; there are not many things that influence the business. There is a sales line, raw materials and labour that give you a prime cost. Then there are some variable overheads, which might be promotional costs, marketing costs, distribution costs, and you've also got contributions to fixed overheads. Then add fixed costs and you've got earnings before interest and tax, you've got some borrowings and you've got an interest bill.

So what do you manage? Yes, you manage sales, you manage efficiencies, variable overheads, and you must know what the profit drivers are. The approach I take is, 'What are the profit drivers on every one of these key elements? If it's cash, what are the debtor days? What is my stockholding? and so on.'

New product development

After a while I started thinking, 'I don't want to be a commodity maker, selling only private label goods, so let's get some branded distribution out there – but brands are expensive, and we don't have big budgets.' I went to the big retailers and asked the obvious question, 'What would it take to make you stock a branded product?' They said, 'It will have to be a different product, that you can't buy from anybody else and I'd want to see it on the television.' I went home, tail between my legs and thought, we can't afford that, can't afford television, but then, what about that lesson you learned years ago that said if you want to achieve something, come what may, you make it happen? So I clicked into that mode because we'd invested in technology for making toffee more cheaply than anyone else in the world – what else can we make, utilising this technology we'd invested in?

We came up with a sugar confectionery, which had a chocolate centre in the middle, and we made it a different shape to anything anyone else had got. Our American distributor said to me, 'I want the packaging different, the harder it is the more I like it, because the competition are put off by trying to copy it or match it.' The shape and metalised twist wrap of this product made it stand out; we persevered, it was really hard to do, but we did it and we put it out in the marketplace, and we built it up as a brand. We had private label houses and major multiple grocers ringing up and saying up they'd like it in their private labels, and we said they couldn't have it. They then said they wouldn't stock it and asked what we would do. I replied that we would go on television to promote it.

We made a very low-cost television commercial, we couldn't afford to put it out nationally, so we did it regionally and the marketing attack was go to the supermarkets and ask for regional distribution in the stores in that area. When we got it there, we put the television advert in and moved it there and when we'd got to a certain momentum within that store and got the distribution up to maybe 25-30 per cent of the stores, proving it was selling well, the rest was relatively easy. We didn't set ourselves a limiting budget, we just said, 'Here's a product, we've got to get it in every one of the major multiple grocers and we want it at 100 per cent distribution, look how much margin you can make by rolling this out nationally.'

We knew we were right because there's two things we did: we invested in the technology base to make us the cheapest in the world, relative cost position on toffee, and then the challenge was to maximise this technology commercially, to develop another product, linking into the same technology. We knew the market statistics, we'd done some research on the market, which told us what the size of the sugar confectionery and the chocolate confectionery marketplaces were, we had information which told us about buying characteristics, who bought what – parents buying for children, parents buying for adult consumption, etc. This product was for adult consumption, rather than child consumption.

Nothing's guaranteed, but we did our homework right and had the right relationship with our customer base, the right cost perspective, a good product, and we didn't lose sight of the fact it actually ended up in your mouth, so we were confident that it would succeed. The only thing that's missing is where else do you add value? You add value through relationships between suppliers and customers, so it's all about the job that your people do; if you get that bit right, there's not an awful lot that can go wrong. We costed it to death, we knew what the margins were, we'd looked at what would happen if somebody else tried to get into the marketplace and we knew how difficult that was going to be. Our attitude was, we launch this product, and then we set our stall out to get a new product development programme behind this concept, so that when somebody catches up and launches their product, we've been there, done that and we're doing something else. So it's not rocket science, its all fairly straightforward.

Robert

Questions to Consider in Relation to Turning Round a Business

- How do you go about identifying the causes of underperformance and the potential for growth of an existing business?

- What aspects of the business must be addressed, and what approaches can be used to put these right, in turning round a business?

- What are the essential financial measures that can be used?

- What are the significant personal qualities and skills that the entrepreneur requires to manage a turnaround successfully?

- What can be learned about how to develop and launch a new product successfully from Robert's account?

CHAPTER 7

Moving Out and On from the Business

INTRODUCTION

This chapter aims to explore the ways in which entrepreneurs move out of the ventures with which they have been involved, to discuss what key factors are involved in the process of moving out and on, and how they can be managed successfully.

Moving out of a business can be a difficult process. Whilst it is true that there are entrepreneurs who routinely buy and sell businesses, and whose core activity revolves around investment and divestment decisions, possibly through running a holding company or investment funds, they are relatively few in number. Most entrepreneurs are likely to have been intensively involved with their own business and have been committed to growing it and to making it successful for some considerable time, possibly for most of their working life. At times it may have 'been their life'. There can be much emotional heritage attached to the business. If the business has been family owned, perhaps for several generations, these factors are likely to be even more acute. It can be difficult to value the business objectively.

Yet the reality is that at some point the entrepreneur and the business must part company if the venture is to continue. This is a normal part of the entrepreneurial process and, like the previous phases in the process, it can either be managed poorly, in which case both the entrepreneur and the business are likely to suffer, or it can be managed well. The only exceptions to this are 'lifestyle businesses', and businesses which are so heavily identified and imbued with the personality of the entrepreneur that moving out is simply not an option, they are the business, the business is their career. Entertainment, media and sporting personalities, for example, who may not consider themselves to be entrepreneurs, need to be especially aware of this, however, they will need to be 'moving on', progressing from one form of business venture to another and reinventing themselves as they get older.

The simple fact is that, in most other cases, the entrepreneur must be able to leave a business venture at some time in order to realise the value which they have locked up in it, unless of course they plan to 'die with their boots on'. Viewed in this way, moving out is similar to every other part of the entrepreneurial process: it is about identifying and releasing value. The questions that follow from this include:

- What are the reasons for moving out?
- What is the value of the business?
- To whom is it valuable?

- When to move out?
- How to move out?
- What to do after you've moved out?

Each of these questions will be discussed briefly below, then entrepreneurs' experiences of this phase will be explored.

What are the Reasons for Moving Out?

The reasons may be personal, business, or more likely a combination of the two. You may, for example:

- have grown the business as far as you feel you can and realise that additional capital or other resources are required to enable the business to achieve its potential;
- realise that the business is attractive to buyer(s);
- think the venture has a limited shelf-life;
- be bored and looking for a fresh challenge;
- simply want to retire, or to go and enjoy life (yacht, villa, golf as desired).

It is important to decide what you want, and why. What will it give you?

What is the Value?

The price of the business is likely to depend on the value locked up in the business that the buyer can realise. As with any other asset, it is worth only what someone else is prepared to pay for it at a particular time. This may be determined by such factors as:

- **the price/earnings ratio**: the price is a multiple of the earnings, the post-tax profits of the business, normally taken over a number of years. This ratio can vary greatly, as much as between four and twenty times annual profits, depending on a whole range of factors, notably the industry sector. The business' proven ability to generate cash, its record and prospects for both capital and earnings growth, and the perceived degree of risk (uncertainty) to the buyer will all be highly relevant;
- **the unique capabilities of the business**: these may include intellectual property rights, such as patents, brands, and designs, as well as products, knowledge, skills, information processes, and capacity. How far these are embodied in people (who may choose to leave) or are locked into the business, is likely to be an important factor;
- **market position**: strength in terms of customer loyalty and relationships as well as supplier and distributor relationships;

- **other assets**: including land, property, rights or options which may not have been exercised;
- **the value without the entrepreneur**: this is crucial, the more the principal(s) is closely identified with the business, the more their departure is likely to devalue it.

Professional advice should always be sought in valuing and disposing of businesses. Using capable advisors should mean that advantages, such as a higher price, a smoother sale and reduced personal tax liabilities, may be obtained.

To Whom is it Valuable?

Entrepreneurs should always be wary of accepting the first offer; if there is one, there could be a range of parties interested in the business. These may include:

- competitors;
- entrants to the sector;
- external investors;
- managers and/or other employees in the business;
- customers, suppliers, distributors;
- family members.

When to Move Out?

Timing is crucial. A business is likely to have a peak value depending on the market conditions combined with its performance. By moving out too soon, the full value may not be realised; by leaving it too late, it may start to go stale. There is a degree of opportunism around the exact timing, but planning is essential. Ideally, the exit route should be planned at the entry into the business. Certainly, an entrepreneur should be thinking and planning no less than four to five years ahead, since the financial performance over a number of years will be scrutinised by any buyer. The time taken to sell the business also needs to be planned for, and is likely to take several months once a buyer is found.

The long-term aim should be to maximise the exit value and price of the business. Therefore, aiming to enhance its attractiveness and value should form a key part of the growth strategy for the business. This goal should guide the investment policy in the business; by investing in aspects of the business which will both enhance its growth capability and its eventual value.

The entrepreneur should move towards ensuring that all key aspects of the business are 'in good working order' and will stand up to external inspection by experts. This may take months or even years to achieve. Below are some of the key areas that will need to be considered and may need to be worked on.

- **Finances**: balance sheet and accounts up to date, no black holes or surprises, everything must be explicit, any liabilities quantified.
- **Legal issues**: rights, contracts, deeds and insurance must be documented and verifiable.
- **People**: are there operational managers and personnel who will stay with the business?
- **Products, processes and procedures**: are these working effectively, documented and specified? Management systems, such as ISO 9000, are of considerable value here.
- **Information and records**: are they organised and retrievable?
- **Capital items, plant and equipment and stocks**: these are auditable.

In short, the business needs to be demonstrably under control, with no factors that might cause doubt or uncertainty.

How to Move Out?

There are a number of options for exit, which will depend on the issues summarised so far as well as on the entrepreneur's stake in the business. Assuming that you, as the entrepreneur, own some equity in the business, do you own it all, and what involvement (if any) do you wish to continue to have in the business? Listed below are the main options.

- **Liquidation, realising the sale value of the tangible assets to repay creditors.** This is the worst exit route of all, and is included here as an 'awful warning' since so many small businesses (and occasionally bigger ones) end up being liquidated, often with derisory value being extracted from them. Do not fall into this trap.
- **A trade sale to a competitor or market entrant, either as a takeover or possibly as a merger.** This may attract a satisfactory or better price depending on the timing but do not look for any continued involvement in the business.
- **Sale to a management buy-in (MBI).** The process may be prolonged.
- **Sale to buy-out from existing managers (MBO) or, indeed, from an employee buy-out.**
- **A combined management buy-in and buy-out (BIMBO).**

Any of the last four options given above may be attractive. The credibility of the buyer(s) and their ability to finance a satisfactory purchase price are clearly vital.

- **Leaving or selling the business to family member(s).** Again this needs planning and professional advice; ensuring the family member(s) are ready to succeed, and that there are processes in place to transfer ownership which are acceptable to all parties, avoiding disputes over shares, rewarding you and minimising tax liability.
- **Flotation, either onto the Alternative Investment Market, in the UK, or exceptionally a full Stock Exchange flotation.** These routes are for exceptional businesses only. They are costly and there is often a high degree of risk in the success of the flotation and in subsequent share performance. High, sustained growth rates are essential together with a clear plan of how the flotation will enable growth and performance to improve further. Flotation should really form part of an entrepreneur's exit strategy, by providing considerable personal wealth and a public valuation of the business, since successful entrepreneurs are not always seen as 'safe hands' by the City. Fashion may also play a part, for example biotechnology businesses being attractive to the market one year, but near impossible to float once Internet businesses have become the next 'flavour of the season'.

As well as planning their own exit, it is essential to consider the managers and employees in the business. The departure of the principal(s) will affect them. It is hard to conduct sale negotiations secretly, especially once strange men in suits start going round counting things, as they will. It is better to be up-front about the future intentions for the business. As businesses become more knowledge and people-dependent, consider what the implications of divestment plans may mean for them. A demotivated and disappearing workforce will do nothing for the performance and value of the business. Customers and suppliers are then likely to find out, which also tends to damage business prospects. There are strong arguments for management and employee equity ownership but this needs to be implemented in good time and for the right reasons.

Finally, the entrepreneur needs good advice to minimise their personal tax liability on the sale proceeds. For example, the UK government is liberalising capital gains tax liability for entrepreneurs realising the value of their equity, subject to various conditions.

What to Do after you've Moved Out?

There is life beyond the venture: it is up to you to decide what form it takes. There are two basic questions here.

What are your aims and motivators?

The issues here are the same as were covered in Chapters 1 and 2; What do you want to achieve, and why? But having moved on from at least one venture, the options available are probably broader. They may include:

- **enjoying a good lifestyle in semi or full-retirement**: if you've been successful enough and had enough of business. But do you *really* want to just play golf every day?;
- **do it again as a serial entrepreneur**: find another venture, grow it, realise the value, move out;
- **leverage your expertise**: become involved in helping other businesses succeed. This could be in one of several roles, which may overlap:
  - business angel/investor;
  - non-executive chairman or director;
  - mentor and advisor;
- **taking up a public governance role**: on an expert body or one such as Regional Development Agencies, NHS Trust or in education: but you may have to live with 'red tape'!

What is your value?

You have to be clear what you are best at, what you enjoy doing and what you want to get out of it. It may be a combination of 'putting something back into the community', feeling one's experience is valued by others, and being able to profit or be rewarded for what you do. Your value may, for example, be in:

- **entrepreneurial ability**: helping other businesses to grow;
- **having a proven ability in turnarounds**;
- **expertise and specialist knowledge**: which may be market, technical or business-related, such as in finance, acquisitions or mergers;
- **as an investor** with a more active or passive involvement as desired.

Moving on successfully involves doing many of the things (which have already been addressed in earlier chapters in this book) in a different context. There are traps for the unwary. Do not assume that, just because you have 'done it before' that you can automatically repeat the same golden formula and do it again. Every situation is different. Below are some points to remember.

- Every potential opportunity you consider needs to be appraised thoroughly ('Assessing Opportunities', Chapter 3).
- What is the fit between your aims, capabilities, experiences, resources and the investment proposition? Does your experience in one context translate into a different one?
- Are you prepared to invest time, money or both? How much of each, for how long, and what return do you expect to gain?

- Can you trust the people involved? Why are you being asked: beware of the vanity trap of giving support to a venture that could damage your reputation. Check it and the people involved out carefully.
- A non-executive role can be very different from that of the entrepreneur driving the business. It is catalytic, about achieving change and results through others. It is not, fundamentally, your business even though you may have a stake in it. It means combining providing value for the executives with exercising responsibility and sometimes restraint. And it is best to avoid a 'when I was...' attitude of having seem and done it all before which others may find patronising. Every business is unique in some way, and the market and technological environment at the end of the 20th and early in the 21st centuries are quite different conditions for businesses from those you may have experienced before.

Exercise

What are your questions about moving out of the venture? Note them down before reading the entrepreneurs' accounts of this process.

THEMES

Below several of the entrepreneurs we encountered in Chapters 5 and 6 describe their experiences of moving out and on from businesses they have grown successfully.

- Preparing to move out – why, when and how?
- After you've moved on – what to do next?
- The importance of trust.

Preparing to Move Out: Why, When, How?

Anna explained her vision for the next phase of her career in terms of transition, of realising the value in the business and moving on.

We are a successful company, making very good profits, we're a very desirable company to people, we have had approaches and we have said 'no, no, no'. I think it will be our plan to sell and then do what, I don't know. My husband's decided he would take up golf full-time and never do a day's work again in his life and I'm sat there thinking 'I can't do this' so the plan is to sell to capitalise on everything that we've got. We are certainly in a position where we will never have to work again, but that's not the motivation now. The motivation to work is not the money any more – at sixteen it was, now it's the whole sense of the achievement, goals, everything about it. It is no longer the money side and I don't know what we are going to do. I'd certainly have to do something else, and I will do something else, maybe something totally different from the business we are in but what that something else is yet I'm not quite sure.

Anna

This is characteristic of an entrepreneur who has successfully built a business and realises that the optimum time to sell may be close but who is considering the personal issues of what to do next. The driving forces have changed, the motivation now is achievement rather than money, and the considerations expressed are personal rather than for the business. Linda's concerns, however, rather than being personal are very much for the future of her business and especially its people.

We are planning now a long time in advance for when we leave because we want the people to have job security for life. We've built something we want to carry on. We would love a management buy-out and we are starting now because we believe in long-term planning, we believe in long-term goals, and if we communicate those goals now, it's not going to be a culture shock when one day we don't turn in because we have retired. They have got to know we are so committed to them, we are like a family. We will grow, we see security as being in growth but we want to consolidate, we want to hand over a company that has got environmental, people and quality accreditation, we want to be the best at what we do. It doesn't mean we have to be the biggest, but we want to be the best and to have all the mechanisms in place so that, however we exit, we hand over a very good company to whoever we hand it over to, and that there is security in the long-term for everybody involved.

Linda

The concern for the continuity and security of the workforce here are commendable and reflect the owners' long-term planning and continued commitment, but should not stand in the way of their being fully rewarded for the work they have put into creating and growing a successful business. It is likely to be harder to move out of a business you have started and built yourself than one you have acquired, and the next account from David forecasts the exit routes he contemplated from an early stage in the turnaround of the business he had bought into.

I genuinely believe that, through the efforts that we are putting in over a 5-year period, we'll probably be able to treble the profits of this business and you can then work out the exit route from there, whether it be that you float it, because it's worth investing in and we can get some public investment into the business because it looks good and people will want a share of it. Or, alternatively, there may be a large US nursery player who

*wants to break into the UK market and they want a vehicle ready made to
get in there which has already got the doors open and that becomes an
acquisition route. Or it may be a competitor who wants to buy us out of
the way. Whatever the route, the key I'm sure is building the right image
and having a cleverly, slickly and properly run company.*

He also reflected on the personal rewards of managing one of these exit
routes successfully.

*I've always been judged on results and I've never been unhappy about
that, the results of making this happen can be very lucrative for me. I
mean that's the difference, it's not going to be just a salary increase or a
bonus or whatever, it could be extremely lucrative, so there's a real desire
to make it work.*

David

At this stage, David is aware of the various exit options, the pay-off for
the sheer graft required to turn round and transform the business, and
the success criteria he will need to hit to make the business as attractive
as possible for the exit route. The route itself can be decided nearer the
time. The presence of venture capital investors, and the fact that they
will look for a highly profitable capital gain from the exit, will tend to
act as a further motivator in this situation. However, there is no doubt
that the prospect of personal gain can be a powerful incentive in moving
out of a business. Here is Robert's description of how he sold the confectionery business that was featured in Chapter 6.

*Suddenly the word came from the owners, 'We're not going to compete on
buying businesses – milk this company for all it is worth.' So, I thought,
'That's not really what I'm here to do.' But I did it for a few months and
then walked into the chairman's office and said, 'I don't want to be doing
this for the foreseeable future, why don't we sell the business to somebody
who will invest in it?' He said, 'OK, we want £x million for the business
– go and sell it and here's a financial incentive for you to beat it.' That
taught me how turned-on I was by earning money, big-buck style. I went
out and found an organisation that would buy into the strategic plan that
we had in place, including the capital investment required to deliver it,
and I thought right, there's one thing missing here, that's some ackers for
me, how can I get some money out of this on this bonus incentive? I did it
by selling it for twice the target and earned the biggest bonus I've earned
in my life, and I met all the other commercial business criteria.*

Robert

Although Robert initially stayed with the business, he moved on shortly afterwards. The senior manager, who is an employee without an

equity stake or share options, may have an exalted position in the business but lacks both ultimate control over the ownership and destiny of the business and the prospect of significant personal reward for its growth. This helps to explain the interest shown over recent years by career executives in management buy-ins and buy-outs, as they realise that the rewards – not only financial – from entrepreneurial success can be greater than those in corporate life.

In some ways, an opposite journey may be travelled by successful entrepreneurs who float their businesses. Three entrepreneurs who gained high profiles in the UK during the 1980s, Richard Branson, Alan Sugar and Anita Roddick, each had stormy experiences with corporate investors after flotation. A different set of expectations – from institutional investors, City analysts, commentators and financial journalists – start to kick in after flotation. The entrepreneur is no longer 'their own boss', but is answerable to a new, and often quickly critical, set of stakeholders. It may be that this is the stage when the individualistic entrepreneurs, who built the business and have been accustomed to a very personalised style of direction, need to head towards the exit, to be replaced by corporate managers who will be able to reassure institutional investors. The next account, by Brian, recounts how his business was floated on the Unlisted Stock Market in the late-1980s. It subsequently achieved full Stock Exchange listing.

> *We were very lucky in a sense, because it was just in time. It was obvious that we had to do something because things couldn't go on forever like that. We knew we wanted to do something and retrospectively it is quite clear to me that we should have sold because if you float you have to expand much more rapidly than you have done before. I was all for it because I thought it was about time we got going and really started taking over other people, the greenfield site days were gone. This would give us a platform to do it from.*
>
> *But as we started to come out of the recession, I realised that my colleagues didn't want to take over other companies. One of them subsequently changed but one in particular just didn't want to and I then desperately worked at getting the business sold, which I eventually succeeded in doing. Certainly, as far as I was concerned, the flotation was so that we could really start to accelerate our growth. It was a mistake for the three of us, but we still managed to keep the thing going quite well and I have now finally sold out of the business. I believed I wanted to float. I worked towards changing things, but you cannot float and expect to trundle along as you have previously.*
>
> Brian

This describes how the conflicting aims and expectations among the three directors, which had existed since the early days of the business, re-emerged and were unresolved. This story does indicate the need for an agreed growth strategy to follow from the flotation. Firm control and clear direction are essential, since 'drift' and indecision are quickly picked up on by City analysts and affect the share price.

The final account here is by John, describing his reasons for moving out of an executive role in the retail business. This account is the culmination of a long process of organic growth, acquisition, merger, and repeated rejuvenation of this business over more than 25 years. He had brought into the business and developed people who were able to take over the management and structured a deal which enabled him to move into a non-executive role.

> *In the firm now, the management are good, better than me, they are more talented than I am. That's wonderful because you just let them get on with it and go and do something else. But it is unusual because, generally speaking, people do not develop to be better than you, it is a myth because it's the old elephant herd syndrome, you keep the young bulls down as long as you can and then, when they kill you or beat you, off you go.*
>
> *One of the things that I enjoy in life is developing people and developing businesses. That's why when the family firm got to be so large, I just got bored and then I got back down to what I considered to be small businesses, where you can still relate to all the individuals in the company.*
>
> John

After you've Moved On: What to do Next?

In this final section, we look at the experiences of three entrepreneurs after they had moved on from the business they had grown.

After leaving the confectionery business, Robert worked on turning round a series of underperforming food sector businesses. But after completing one such project for a major food group, he reflected:

> *This started me thinking, I've been made redundant for the first time in my life, this is never going to happen to me again. The way I'll make that not happen is by having equity in a business and I will become a shareholder, so I went down that route. I decided I wanted equity, come what may I'm going to do it.*
>
> Robert

He went on the management buy-in trail, and identified several potential acquisitions, raised venture capital and aimed to complete the deal – but on each occasion it failed. As we have seen in Chapter 5, this is not unusual. After some time, he was invited to take an equity stake as

MD of a snack food business, which had previously been bought out from a food group. He described his aims for the venture a few months after joining.

> *I achieved my ambition of getting equity status, although a much small-er one than I was pursuing. But I am my own boss here and I am the only executive member of the board, there are three non-executive direc-tors on the board, and I'm running it, I'm loving it, I enjoy the business.*
>
> *I want to add value to everything I do, to people, to the products and to our business plan. I'm conscious that this is a private company and shareholders look for an exit, and the exit will either be flotation or a sale. I'm interested in adding value by going out and getting into new but related sectors either by buying something and bolting it on, or doing a new product start-up, bolting it on and piggy backing and forc-ing out the synergies which grow the business. I'm turned on by max-imising that exit, not only for selfish reasons because I've got some money to make here myself, but maximising returns for the people that have shown faith in the business by putting their money in. Whether that's flotation or sale it's maximising that return and getting it right.*
>
> *Now, at that stage, I want to make sure that there is a good future in the business for the people here, and that they have got security. For myself, I'm open minded depending on what the exit route is, whether I stay on with it, maybe I'll be part of the exit, maybe I'll buy it – who knows, that is certainly in my mind as a secondary buy-out. But if I'm not part of the future, once the exit comes I'll go and look for something else and do it all over again.*
>
> Robert

Robert's hands-on approach shows total commitment to making the business as successful as possible for as long as he is running it – for the owners, the people and, of course, himself – and a clarity about the options for growing and exiting from the business. Although commit-ted to the venture he is also able to detach himself from its future if that is the best exit option and to go off and grow another underperforming business. One senses that his preference will be an executive role where he is able to drive change through and make things happen. The two entrepreneurs we now turn to have chosen a different, non-execu-tive role and we follow their accounts of how this developed.

Since moving out of the equipment hire business, Brian has developed interests in other growing enterprises including a hi-tech start-up in the acoustics field, as a partner in an estate and property management agency, and as a mentor to the management team in another business.

> *I like the idea of helping small organisations to grow. I like the idea of helping people with good ideas to work at that idea and I'll take care of*

the commerce for them. I'm just about to be appointed chairman of an acoustic company, which has a world lead in surround sound. We are seeking ways of raising large sums of money so that we can really expand this business. Now that is fascinating, perhaps it won't work, but it really has the potential to do so. I bring some respectability to these young people in open necked shirts and stubble and that's what I like. I can avoid them having to waste their time on the commercial side of things. I like building things, I'm not into meetings which are isolated from the work of the business, where you simply pore over the figures. I'm into what people do, not necessarily what they make, just what they do, that's what motivates me. I've got a share option with this company and if we build it up in the right way that will quite a lot of money within a reasonable time.

Brian described his approach as a non-executive as one of concentrating the managers' minds on *'getting things right'*.

When I go into a business I say 'this is not rocket science but you can't afford to get things wrong, you don't have to be brilliant but you've got to get everything right' and that's what it is about. You do have to get things right and it is the job of the people at the top to decide how things should be done and it is also their job to listen. They've got to say 'this is how we will do things', and people then have to do it that way.

If you are young, you do need the right sort of mentor. There is a dynamic young man I know who runs an estate agency. There is no way he could ever be an employee or have a partner, he's much too autocratic. But I am no threat to him. I'm always there at the end of the phone, he phones me up and says, 'What are we going to do about this?' He then talks for about fifteen minutes and I say three words while he just talks it through to himself. I think that people of my age have something to offer young people because of our experience and I think that is very important. Most entrepreneurs have some sort of mentor.

Brian

Several things emerge from this narrative. One is that Brian's motivation seems to be two-fold: it is about helping younger people to do the right things to grow their businesses and to *'meet the challenges'* successfully. It also continues to be about making money because this motivates and brings him satisfaction. But from his description of advising and mentoring young entrepreneurs, showing them *'how to get everything right'*, there is a strong sense of him enabling them to learn; of entrepreneurship as 'living theory' which is made up of the collected experiences, meanings and wisdom of the successful entrepreneur who, having learned them for himself, is passing them on to the next generation of entrepreneurs. In this way, we can understand entrepreneurial learning as a continuing process of individuals learning from their own and others' experiences, developing their own 'theories of business' within their own venture, and having proved to be successful in applying their theories, enabling others to learn from them.

From this, we can recognise the value for the young business of having an experienced, trusted and successful advisor/mentor who is able to help them to learn. Mark commented on the value which the two non-executive directors brought to his engineering business.

> *They have got a lot of experience I would never hope to have at my age and I accept the fact that I had no experience of running a business. I've got the technical expertise but you need something else and for that you've got to bring people in, and it works really well.*
>
> Mark

However, it must not be assumed that, even for the highly successful entrepreneur, becoming a successful non-executive chairman or director is either easy or bomb-proof. It is a learning journey in itself. Following his executive career in building up a retail business, John went on to develop a portfolio of non-executive interests in such fields as engineering, education, design and a café bar chain. Here he candidly recounts his initial difficulties.

> *I can be very stubborn and when I became a non-executive director, I identified certain areas that I wanted to be involved in where I had absolutely no experience or knowledge. I was determined to do it against all the advice, and I was wrong. I got completely and utterly enthused with the concept and I didn't use my usual analysis. I thought I was right but I got it completely wrong, and I had to work jolly hard to retrieve the company and get it back on a stable basis. It was sheer stubbornness, forgetting all the things that I have believed in. It was an arrogance that I've got a good track record, I know what I am doing and I'm determined that this is going to be right in an area I knew nothing about.*
>
> John

Clearly, there are dangers in assuming one's own theory of business can be transferred readily into unfamiliar sectors. Also, 'due diligence' is needed on the business itself, to find out about it and the people involved in it, and what they are seeking from your involvement. Finally, it seems that becoming an effective non-executive involves learning to perform the role successfully, but there is much less time, and the tolerance for mistakes is lower – you are expected to be right, that is what you are there for. John commented on how his speed of learning and thinking aided his effectiveness as a non-executive.

I learn quickly, it is that ability to learn and absorb fast. In the car going to the board meeting, I will be reading my board papers. I absorb it very fast, and I can identify the problems very quickly and that's experience I suppose.

As Brian recounted, John has also come to make judgements about the businesses with which he will work on the basis of how compatible he feels he is with the people running the business, as well as on the potential of the business itself.

Now my criterion is: 'Is the chief executive somebody who I can work with and develop this business, or, if he isn't, do I know somebody that I can do it with?' The businesses that I am now involved in have the characteristic that the people are the kind I like to work for and with, and I am not really bothered about the sector. It's the people that I find fascinating, because I have not got the original idea. I am not the merchant, or the scientist, or the computer technician, but I can find somebody who can develop that company and show it how to grow. So I am not the original ideas man, but I like working with people that have got that flow, I find it stimulating and what I find even more stimulating is showing them how to realise their ambitions.

John

It is again the non-executive's role in *'showing them how to grow'* that is significant; both rewarding to the experienced entrepreneur and of great help to the younger people running the business. As John recounts, they tend to come from specialist backgrounds – engineer, merchant, scientist or computer technician as the case may be – and have not yet developed the breadth of business understanding that is needed to optimise the growth of their business, but which they can draw from the experienced mentor. The learning, and consequent change, that he imparts may be something quite simple and apparently *'obvious'* but which is, nonetheless, missing until the non-executive, with a fresh pair of eyes, causes the people running the business to make a small change which can have quite a dramatic effect on performance. Here John describes how he played a catalytic role in getting the team in one business to communicate more effectively.

I get a terrific buzz, particularly if they are young. I was asked to get involved in a small design company. I know nothing about design but it was formed four years ago by a group of young people. The figures were wonderful, the accounting was terrific, everything was wonderful. The one thing they didn't do, they just didn't talk to each other. The managing director was getting frustrated because the sales director was not getting any orders, so I said, 'Have you told her?' He said, 'No, that's her job, that's what the specification says.' I replied, 'Have you actually sat down and said to her we need some orders in three weeks time otherwise we have got no work?' 'No.' So I called her across, and said, 'Do you know that in three weeks time you are all going to be sitting around doing nothing?' She replied, 'No, but I've got some wonderful orders for next year.' I said, 'You're not going to get to next year, so on a Monday morning instead of coming in at 9 am come in at 8.30 am and all sit down and tell each other what you did last week, and what you are going to do this week.' This has helped the business. Now for me that was a wonderful thing because they were this bunch of immensely talented kids who were missing one vital ingredient, which I gave them, and that company will go on to be successful.

John

Again, we see a live process of learning being enacted in this episode; the young team might well have discovered from experience that they needed to communicate face to face, but they would have lost ground whilst doing so, possibly even putting the business at risk. However, the experienced mentor was able to short-circuit the process and immediately enabled them to learn a more effective way of working.

The Importance of Trust

All three of the entrepreneurs, whose experiences are recounted in this section, commented on the importance of trust in working with people, and also on the converse; in moving outside the familiarity of their own businesses, the difficulty in knowing who to trust, and the danger of being let down. Here Robert recounts what happened during one management buy-in, which he aborted when the vendor misled them.

I found a niche food manufacturing business with nice margins, very profitable, not a turnaround and I got venture funding, it was all in place. Two weeks off the completion meeting, having worked on it for six months, and not having an income, something came out of the woodwork that they had not disclosed to us which was earth shattering. I went to the venture capitalist and said, 'We shouldn't pursue this now, I've got no trust and confidence in the management, and if they've lied to us about this what else have they lied about? So hard as it may be we don't go for it.' And we walked away.

Robert

This incident of course highlights the need for full disclosure by vendors of businesses as well as due diligence by buyers; skeletons in the cupboard will emerge sooner or later. It also reinforces a key plank of Robert's theory of business:

Don't take everything that everybody tells you at face value – question it.

Robert

Next, Brian describes how his intuitive and informal approach to doing business – to agree verbally, then act – has sometimes left him exposed as his role changed.

Trust has always been a big thing for me and I've made mistakes. I hate to be in business with people I can't trust. I don't want to sign contracts, I want to do things with people. I say, 'I'll do this,' and they say, 'Yes OK, you do that and I'll do this.' Then we do it. It left me very exposed when the business was taken over, because I trusted the person. I thought he was a friend but I learnt the difference between friendship and friendliness. I did learn from that, that I had to choose my bed fellows very carefully because I am only interested with people with very solid integrity. There's another thing I instinctively knew and learned.

Brian

Again, we see the entrepreneur's instinctive knowledge of what is right being confirmed through an unpleasant experience, reinforcing his business theory of dealing only with people with solid integrity.

John describes how the entrepreneur's reputation is of value both to himself but also to others. But once away from the network of familiar relationships, it is dangerous to assume that people running other businesses can be trusted to the same extent.

One enjoys a reputation, that reputation is important to you, you do favours for people, and help with developing small companies.

I have been used to working with people that I trust because I have helped them and we have a mutual need for each other. I think that there have been areas in which I have assumed that other people I have gone into business with have been as trustworthy as the people that I have known for longer or developed or whatever, and very often that is not reciprocated, and that's just life.

John

REVIEW

Take a few minutes to reflect on the questions you posed at the start of this chapter on the process of moving out of and on from the venture.

CONCLUSION

This concludes the three chapters that have aimed to give an understanding of the entrepreneurial process through the narratives of entrepreneurs themselves. Through posing questions to structure our own inquiry, we are able to make sense of these individual and unique experiences and to form an understanding of the dominant themes, the choices which must be made, and the theories which may be applied to achieve desired results.

So what conclusions can the aspiring entrepreneur draw from these three chapters? Here are three suggestions.

1. **They emphasise the vital role of learning in the entrepreneurial process.** To be successful, continuous learning is essential. That learning can be gained from many sources but what matters is that it is applied to the real task of unlocking value through creating and growing enterprises. The aspiring entrepreneur, therefore, needs to learn constantly, to be consciously aware of what and how they are learning, and to practise using what they have learned. The entrepreneurial learning model (see Chapter 2) sets out the key elements required in a *general* way; you as an individual need to make it *specific* to encapsulate your own unique learning resources and abilities.

2. **Entrepreneurship is living theory.** It is embodied in the experiences, conclusions and personal theories of individuals who have practised it successfully. The aspiring entrepreneur can, therefore, learn greatly from the experience and guidance of mentors who themselves have substantive achievement. Seek out people you think you can learn from; even a little of their time can be highly stimulating. If you can get to know them better and establish a learning relationship, so much the better. But in the end the development of your own theory of business, which works for you in achieving the results you want, is a necessary goal.

3. **Entrepreneurship is about doing, and learning from doing.** So the question must be, if you have not yet started, what are you going to do? That leads us into the final chapter, which aims to help you to plan your entrepreneurial career and to start to enact it.

CHAPTER 8

Planning your Entrepreneurial Career

The aim of this chapter is to help you apply the essential lessons from this book when planning how to develop your own entrepreneurial career. It brings together the themes of previous chapters and asks you to focus on the following key questions.

- What do you want to achieve, and why?
- What is your personal value? How can you unlock and increase this?
- How will you accomplish your goals?
- What do you need to learn in order to achieve your goals?
- How will you gain this learning?

The approach taken in this chapter is to encourage you to think reflectivly about what has been learned from the exercises in the book; to bring together your conclusions and to use them in creating a plan for your future; and then to go forward and to make it happen. The outcome of the chapter is, therefore, that you prepare a career plan for yourself. If you have already done this, the chapter will give you an opportunity to revisit and reflect on it with some fresh insights. Most people do not have a career plan, and here are some reasons why you, as an aspiring entrepreneur, should have one.

- A plan puts you in control; you direct where you want to go.
- A career plan is your personal business plan; your entrepreneurial career is your core business and a plan will help you to manage it effectively.
- Planning enables you to create new scenarios and possibilities and to think through how to achieve them as well as working out how to solve problems before they arise.
- The plan will help you to unlock, increase and retain your individual value in all senses – personal, business and financial.

Before starting this chapter, there are some resources that it will be helpful to have around which arise from the work you have done in Chapters 2, 3 and 4. Here is a list of those resources.

Chapter 2
Unlocking Personal Value   Learning preferences.
                                  Your life story.
                                  Personality preferences.
                                  Relationships and contacts.
                                  Your map of entrepreneurial learning.

Chapter 3
Unlocking External Value   The exercises on a possible venture: identifying,
                                  creating, assessing and deciding, designing and
                                  planning the business.

Chapter 4
Connecting Personal   Decision map of a growth strategy.
and Business Goals   Business goals and indicators.

(Appendix 1)   Skillcheck questionnaire.

(Appendix 3)   Opportunity assessment questionnaire.

In developing your career plan, you will revisit much of this information. You may find that a lot of the thinking is already there, but the planning process will help you to think it through, to bring it together, and to decide what you will do and how to make it a reality.

The career planning process has five headings, as shown in the following map. Each of these five headings is then explored through a series of questions, which are intended to prompt you to think through each aspect and to help you to develop your career plan around it.

Figure 8.1: Your career plan

YOUR CAREER PLAN

Select the preferred format for your career plan: this could be as a mind map, a table-type plan (there is a format in Appendix 4), a narrative or whatever format works best for you.

You will find that there are many interconnections between the headings of the plan. Although the five headings used here are a suggestion, you can develop your own if you prefer. It could be, for example, that you create financial, learning and venture plans which lock into the career plan. In each of the five sections, start to develop your career plan, based on the work you have already done and on the further thinking which you do in response to the questions posed.

Goals and Motivations

In Chapter 2, we explored personal goals, values and motivations quite deeply. Revisit this thinking and reflect on it.

- What do you now consider your motivating forces to be?
- What are the values that are most important to you?
- Do you have a personal vision for your future? If so, what is it? If you have not yet developed a personal vision, try using the 'forethought' exercise in Chapter 2 to do this.
- What are your goals for:
  - business;
  - career;
  - personal growth;
  - family;
  - social.
- For each of these goals, think about how you will measure or assess when you have achieved it.

Increasing Personal Value

An important theme of this book is unlocking both personal and external value to create new opportunities. As a career philosophy, it is about unlocking and growing your personal value over your lifetime. Your value takes a number of different forms: your value to yourself and to others as a person, the value of your capabilities, know-how and reputation, your financial value, and so on; the list could be much longer. The key point here is to assess your current value, under the headings that are most important to you, and to decide how and to what level you want to increase your value.

- How do you assess your own self-worth?
- What do you consider is your greatest value to other people?

- From the exercises in Chapter 2, think back and consider what you would assess your personal value to be in terms of your:
  - capabilities;
  - know-how;
  - personality.
- How do you consider you can use these qualities most effectively to develop your career?
- In what ways do you aim to increase or develop these qualities further?

Let us now consider the financial aspects, a vital measure for most entrepreneurs.

- What is your total net financial worth? You can work this out by estimating the value of your main assets, such as property, business equity, investments and savings, pension plan, valuable possessions and ready cash, and deducting your liabilities – debt, mortgage, etc.
- How satisfied are you with this value?
- At present day values, to what figure do you aim to increase your net assets, and by when? If you plan to retire at a given age, how much personal wealth do you aim to generate by then? How many times can you aim to multiply your present value? The younger you are, the higher the multiple of your current wealth this can be.
- How much of your personal wealth are you prepared to invest in your own business venture, given the risks and potential returns?
- What is your current annual income, after tax and deductions?
- How satisfied are you with this figure, which is the current financial value placed on your work?
- To what figure do you aim to increase this next year? In two years? In ten years? Again, use present day values for this.

These questions should help you to generate some financial targets that quantify your goals.

Ventures

In Chapter 3, you developed some ideas around one possible opportunity, assessed its potential as a venture and as an investment proposition, and started planning it as a possible venture. For an entrepreneur, as shown in Chapters 4-7, it is their successful involvement in entering, growing and exiting these ventures that accomplishes their goals and realises their personal value.

Looking at your personal expectations in terms of goals, motivations and financial targets, think about the optimum route to achieving these.

- If you continue to do what you are currently doing, will this enable you to achieve your aspirations?

If the answer is 'yes' then you are fortunate (or possibly complacent?) and you do not really need to continue with this. If the answer is 'no', then continue below.

- My aspirations will be best achieved through:
  - a salaried career role in an organisation;
  - becoming a manager with an equity share in a business;
  - investing in an existing business, with or without a management role;
  - creating and growing my own business;
  - improving the returns from what I do now;
  - another route not described above.

Different options will be the best ones at different stages of a career. For example, the first option may not seem very entrepreneurial, however, for a younger person at the start of their career, it may be the best way of building up experience, capabilities, contacts and financial resources to prepare for an entrepreneurial move after a few years.

Whichever option you have chosen, you need to plan for it. If you are seeking a management role with an equity stake, unless that can be achieved in your current organisation you will need to search for a suitable opportunity. If you are looking to acquire or invest in an existing business, again you need to decide on your investment criteria and to start searching.

If you intend to create your own venture, then researching and preparing a business plan as outlined in Chapter 3 is essential. There are many other books and sources of help on this.

If the option of improving the returns from what you do now is the one you have chosen, this suggests that you work in a business which is either your own or you share in the profits in some way. It is likely that you need to identify opportunities from which your business can unlock value. Revisit Chapter 3 to look at how you can identify and exploit such opportunities. Aim to identify at least one project that is a sound investment proposition, and develop a plan to exploit it.

Personal Learning

None of this can be realised without effective learning; applying what you have already learned, as well as learning new capabilities and developing new theories.

Look at the goals you have set yourself, and the ventures you plan to run which will achieve your goals.

- Entrepreneurial capabilities (from the Skillcheck in Appendix 1).
  - Personal organisation.
  - Technical capability.
  - Interpersonal skills.
  - Venture planning.
  - Marketing and selling.
  - Financial management.

At the end of the Skillcheck there are suggested ways in which you can develop each skill set further. Then look at your self-analysis from Chapter 2.

- From your life story, your capabilities and know-how.
- Personal theory: what works for you.
- Learning style and personality preferences.

There is a lot here! You need to consider the following questions.

- Does your learning, up to this point, provide you with all the personal capabilities and knowledge you will need to accomplish the business venture you are planning?
- What further learning do you therefore need in relation to this venture?
- Looking at your personal goals overall, does your current learning provide you with all the capabilities and knowledge you will need to achieve them?
- What further learning do you think you need in order to achieve your goals?

List your areas for personal learning and development. For each of them, think about the areas listed below.

- What do you need to learn, is it to develop capabilities, knowledge, understanding?
- Why is the learning important? What could the consequences of 'not learning' be?
- When do you need to have learned by? What are the priorities?
- How can you gain the learning you need?
- Based on these questions, what do you think your learning goals are?

The final section in this chapter includes suggestions on learning that will help you to prepare a learning plan as part of your career plan. As Winston Churchill is rumoured to have said:

If you think education is expensive, try ignorance!

Building Networks

In Chapter 2, you drew a map of your relationships and contacts, and considered how your network could help you in a venture. At this stage of planning your career, how could people in your existing network be of help to you – for example, by:

- investing or providing other resources;
- buying from you or supplying you;
- opening access to people, knowledge, resources;
- helping you learn and develop, e.g. as a mentor.

Your network forms an important resource, and, like any investment, it will be more valuable if it is well managed. So in addition to thinking about its current uses, think about:

- How can you sustain your network of contacts to promote their future co-operation? Who could be your future customers and investors? There are likely to be particular contacts you will wish to cultivate – that is why bank managers used to receive bottles of whisky at Christmas!
- How can you grow your network? Do you need to develop more contacts in specific domains, such as high-level industry contacts, investors, etc.?

We have now completed the five headings of the career plan. Take time out to develop your own career plan in your chosen format. You may find that this takes several attempts; what is important is that you create the plan which you believe in and which you are fired up to go out and turn into reality.

PLANNING YOUR LEARNING AND DEVELOPMENT

Since learning is such an integral aspect of entrepreneurial achievement, the following section is included to give you additional ideas and summarises some of the options open to you for developing the learning aspects of your career plan. It is subdivided into three types of learning methods.

- **Active**: learning through practice.
- **Social**: learning from others.
- **Formal**: theoretical learning.

Figure 8.2: Entrepreneurial capability: sources of learning

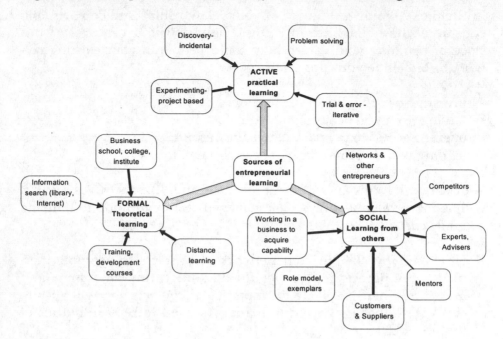

Active Learning

This is opportunity or problem-based learning. In establishing a new venture for the first time, for example, the entrepreneur is faced with a set of novel problems and decisions to which they are unlikely to have ready solutions based on their experience. Insights can be gained from formal courses and from other people but even after being guided by these, the entrepreneur must decide and act for himself. Most entrepreneurial learning, in starting and growing a venture, is active and the process of new venture creation is a powerful source of learning.

The results of their decisions and actions – successful or unsuccessful – can be reviewed and learned from. When unsuccessful, another approach is often tried, leading to iterative, trial and error learning. New ventures attempting to generate early sales often follow this pattern, trying one approach then another, until either sufficient sales are achieved, or resources are exhausted and the venture fails. Unfortunately, trial and error learning is often used where, through investigation, the entrepreneur could have found that 'expert' or well-proven approaches to the problem already exist.

Experimenting and 'playing with ideas' – for example, developing a strategy or a new product – generates new insights through discovery learning. This is a powerful process. By working towards a reasonably defined goal, different approaches and combinations can be tried out, going round the learning loop several times until a workable approach is found. Sometimes, there are unexpected outcomes from the discovery process, leading to new possibilities being created.

Learning from Others

Learning is, for most people, a social process, and experience transfer can take many different forms. Early in their careers, many future entrepreneurs develop their core capabilities through working in organisations where they are able to gain the training and experience that enables them to form or acquire a venture later in their career. Getting into dynamic businesses, where you can develop quickly from exceptional people, is an excellent early career move. Working for an entrepreneurial manager or director can be a highly formative, inspirational and sometimes frustrating process.

Networks of business contacts, including other entrepreneurs, industry experts, customers, suppliers and competitors, can be valuable sources of ideas and experiences. Gaining access to such sources of expertise can also be a learning process in relationship-building. Finding out how suppliers and customers operate, and exploring ways of integrating more closely with them, is a rich source of ideas for adding value.

Expert advisors, such as accountants, bankers, lawyers, scientists, academics and business advisors, can often be highly valuable to the entrepreneur as a way of gaining access to expert-based learning. However, the entrepreneur always needs to judge the relevance of the advice to their own situation and its likely efficacy. No advisor is the fount of all knowledge and wisdom, and the entrepreneur needs to assess whether they really understand the business and the problem or are simply offering generalised solutions.

Formal Learning

Can entrepreneurship be taught as academic theory? There is a growing emphasis on teaching entrepreneurship, from schools through to university first and higher degrees, together with many short 'start your own business' courses. The complexity of business together with the need to reduce the high risk of business failure mean that some formal business training is a sensible option for the new entrepreneur.

The experience of leading US business schools is highly influential and has been accompanied by a growing recognition that since the entrepreneurial learning process is highly experiential and opportunity-driven, the teaching process should support this, rather than impose theoretical frameworks.

Developments in distance learning and technology are broadening access to entrepreneurship education, making it easier for people to learn part-time whilst working or running a business and to overcome geographical, time and other barriers. The convergence between entrepreneurship, business education and technology should mean that it becomes easier for the entrepreneur to combine the active learning they gain from starting and growing their business, with formal learning to develop their capability. The use of e-mail and desktop video conferencing make global contact and learning relationships much easier, using technology to access an enriched range of learning with a network of other people.

Finally, information searches to access existing knowledge are becoming more important and easier to conduct. The 'half life' of knowledge in many scientific, technical and business fields is shortening, whilst the ease of access to information through the Internet and related sources, such as online libraries, databases and newsgroups, makes the exchange of knowledge faster. In the era of the knowledge entrepreneur, speedy access to and use of the best available information is essential. Books and media features on entrepreneurs and business ventures are also useful sources of knowledge.

SEVEN SUGGESTIONS FOR MANAGING YOUR CAREER PLAN

1. Think of your plan as a continuously evolving agenda, which is dynamic rather than static, which changes as you learn and progress.
2. Reward yourself for your successes; use each achievement as a motivator to spur you on to greater ones.
3. Encourage yourself to go round the 'learning loop', of doing, reflecting, concluding and planning, engaging your less favoured as well as your preferred learning modes.
4. Try to find someone who is able to be your mentor, such as an experienced entrepreneur who is prepared to listen and coach you through critical moments; this can be immensely valuable.
5. Check regularly how you are progressing against your goals and the plan – review what works for you and what does not, and constantly question and update your personal theory.
6. Learn from achievements but also from setbacks and failure; analyse why they happened, what you could have identified earlier and how to act differently in future.
7. Keep moving forward; search constantly for opportunities to unlock or create value, plan how they can be exploited, and act on those you judge to be the best investments of your resource.

Finally, to close this last chapter of the book here are short quotations from several of the entrepreneurs whose stories we followed earlier in the book. Each of them encapsulate something of 'the entrepreneurial spirit' and they are included here to inspire you to go on to create your own entrepreneurial success story.

I really believe you can do anything if you believe in yourself.

Anna

You can get anywhere that you believe you can, they say that and I reckon its true.

Brian

You think, 'That's where I'm going to get to.' And if somebody puts a block in the way, you just go through it, if you can't get through go round it but you don't let it stop you, come what may you just sort it. If it's hard to do it, then let's just do it a different way, and there's always another way, whatever it is.

Robert

I have got goals in every aspect of my life. Whether you meet them or not doesn't matter, you know you've got the goals and you are more likely to achieve them. We're teleological – you move towards what you think rather than dwell on what you don't want.

Claire

I think you've got to have a belief that this is the way that it's going to be done, and that this is the vision. I know it can be done and we will get there.

David

I think of all the qualities that are needed it is the determination to say, 'That's where I'm going to get to and I will get there.'

John

Appendix 1

SKILLCHECK: ASSESSING YOUR ENTREPRENEURIAL CAPABILITIES

This exercise asks you to assess your level of skill in the key capabilities needed in creating a successful enterprise. Note that we are not talking here of personality traits – 'what kind of person are you' – but of behaviours, 'the things entrepreneurs do in launching a venture'.

It is in the form of a skillcheck with six sections. Each of these includes a cluster of behaviours and skills that are required in each of the following areas.

- Personal organisation.
- Technical capability.
- Interpersonal skills.
- Venture planning.
- Marketing and selling.
- Financial management.

Complete the skillcheck as honestly as you can; this will help the results to be of more value to you. In each cluster, identify the skill areas where you know your capability because you have demonstrated it practically in a real situation. For these skills, score your capability from 1-4 in column 2 as follows.

1 – **Low capability**. I have some knowledge, limited experience.
2 – **Limited capability**. I have moderate experience and knowledge.
3 – **Fairly competent**. I am confident of my ability in most situations.
4 – **Expert**. I am fully capable in all situations.

Mark any skills which you have not had the opportunity to demonstrate by underlining or with a highlight pen. Do not score these.

Total your scores at the end of each section. When you have completed all the sections, plot your scores on the bars at the end of the skillcheck.

Skill Cluster

Personal organisation	Capability
I set personal goals and plan to achieve them.	
I am committed and determined to achieve my goals in the face of adversity.	
I take personal responsibility for actions and their consequences.	
I use time in the most productive ways.	
I believe I can accomplish whatever I set out to achieve.	
I thrive on challenges and uncertainty.	
I make decisions based on facts and analysis not sentiment.	
I resolve problems effectively and speedily.	
Total	

Technical capability	Capability
I have up to date 'expert' skills and knowledge in at least one field where there is a demand.	
I am able to forecast and stay up to date with the latest developments in my field.	
I am able to plan and manage all aspects of the operational process for a venture in my chosen field.	
I am able to produce or provide the product or service myself.	
I am able to ensure customers' requirements for quality, cost and timescale are met.	
I am able to locate and obtain all the materials, technical inputs and information required to produce the product/service.	
I am able to build systems to plan and forecast, monitor and control operations, and record information in the business.	
I am aware of all legislation, statutory requirements and standards which apply to the product or service.	
Total	

Interpersonal skills	Capability
I enjoy meeting new people and making friends.	
I constantly grow and maintain my networks of contacts.	
I am able to find out what is important to people, listen to and understand their points of view.	
I am able to influence and persuade people to accept my point of view.	
I enjoy negotiating and doing deals with people.	
I am able to lead a group and get them to work towards a common goal as a team.	
I am able to coach and develop people to achieve challenging goals.	
I am able to give people feedback, which helps them to improve their performance.	
Total	

Venture planning	Capability
I am able to forecast trends to identify future market needs and opportunities.	
I am able to identify new possibilities for innovative products and services.	
I am able to analyse the strengths, weaknesses, opportunities and threats of a venture.	
I can assess the relative strengths and weaknesses of competitors.	
I am able to plan how to use a product or service to exploit a market opportunity.	
I can identify the critical success factors which will enable the venture to perform effectively in the market.	
I can identify where to obtain all the resources needed to launch a venture: technical, physical, informational, human, financial.	
I am able to prepare an investment proposal for the venture that I can present to potential investors and backers.	
Total	

Marketing and selling	Capability
I am able to identify and segment the characteristics of my target groups of customers in the market.	
I am able to identify the requirements of potential customers through gathering and analysing information to research the market.	
I can plan a campaign to communicate and sell to the target market.	
I can prepare sales promotion tools (e.g. leaflets, adverts, Web pages, proposals) to which customers pay attention.	
I am able to set sales targets and monitor performance against these.	
I am able to contact, meet, present, negotiate with and sell to customers successfully.	
I am able to build and maintain excellent relations with customers.	
I can identify emerging customer needs and plan how they can be met.	
Total	

Managing finance	Capability
I am able to prepare a financial plan for the venture, forecasting income, expenditure and cash flow.	
I am able to establish the working capital finance requirements of the business and find sources of working capital.	
I am able to calculate the sales figures required to breakeven.	
I am able to calculate product prices that will achieve the required profit margin.	
I am able to set expenditure budgets and control these to minimise unnecessary expenditure.	
I am able to negotiate credit terms with suppliers.	
I am able to obtain prompt payment from customers to generate cash.	
I am able to identify and act to minimise risks and potential liabilities to the business.	
Total	

Score Bars

Personal organisation

| 0 | 8 | 16 | 24 | 32 |

Technical capability

| 0 | 8 | 16 | 24 | 32 |

Interpersonal skills

| 0 | 8 | 16 | 24 | 32 |

Venture planning

| 0 | 8 | 16 | 24 | 32 |

Marketing and selling

| 0 | 8 | 16 | 24 | 32 |

Managing finance

| 0 | 8 | 16 | 24 | 32 |

Now look at your scores for each section of the skillcheck. In which sections were your ratings highest? In which sections were they lowest? Use the space below to make a note of these.

	Capability
Highest three clusters	1. 2. 3.
Lowest three clusters	1. 2. 3.

Strengths

The highest three clusters indicate relative strengths in these skill areas. Depending on the degree of strength, they are areas that you should use as foundations for your venture. Look at the skills you have given lower scores in these areas. How can you develop your capability further in these areas? By doing so, you will be able to enhance your potential further. Reflect on how you can use these capabilities to your best advantage. How can they help you overcome the limitations of your weaker areas?

Weaknesses

The lowest three clusters indicate areas of limitation or weakness. These will limit the prospects for your business success and may threaten its survival. Depending on the degree of weakness, you need to act to develop your capabilities in these areas. Pay particular attention to those skills that you have marked as never having practised. These represent areas where you are most vulnerable. Think carefully how you can develop your weaker areas – through formal training, learning from others (for example by seeking out experts in these areas), and gaining practical experience.

Below are some ideas on ways of developing your capabilities in the areas you have identified as being weaker. Have a look at these now and return to them when you start to develop your career plan in Chapter 8.

WAYS OF DEVELOPING YOUR SKILLS

Personal Organisation

- Read personal growth books, such as Stephen Covey's *7 Habits of Highly Effective People*.
- Practise setting goals and managing your time; read a time management book or go on a short course.
- Find someone you can trust who is able to help you as a mentor by listening, supporting and challenging you.
- Encourage people to give you feedback on your progress in changing specific behaviours, which you want to work on, such as concentrating on 'the important' rather than 'the urgent'.
- Reward yourself for when you achieve the goals you set yourself.

Technical Capability

- Stay in touch with people in your industry or profession, e.g. through joining and attending professional institute meetings.
- Take part in 'continuing professional development' seminars and activities.

- Read the latest professional, industry and technical journals.
- Visit 'state of the art' organisations in any sector to learn from leading-edge practices that will quickly become routine.
- Learn how knowledge and information management is being used to transform the best-run businesses.
- Get out of your 'comfort zone' by finding out what happens 'upstream' and 'downstream' of the parts of the supply chain you know best, such as by visiting and working in customer, supplier, partner and even competitor organisations.
- Learn about the areas that you know least about, by spending time with the people who do it every day. This builds up your understanding of such areas as marketing, selling, quality, operations and finance.
- If you manage, learn to do. If you do, learn to manage.
- Train yourself to spot the current problems and future opportunities in your field.

Interpersonal Skills

- Develop your networks of professional and social contacts continuously.
- Talk to and get to know people with different interests, professional and cultural backgrounds from your own, and try to understand their perspectives.
- Develop your public profile by making opportunities to present, discuss, influence and negotiate with people.
- Take a leading role in a group or team and focus the team on defining and achieving its goal.
- Act as a coach or mentor to help others to learn.
- Take opportunities to give other people constructive feedback in learning situations.
- Learn from others whose skills you admire, such as entrepreneurs and leaders, by watching, meeting and talking with them.

Venture Planning

- Analyse and learn from successful – and unsuccessful – ventures that have similarities to your own; identify their strengths, weaknesses, opportunities and threats.
- Read business plans and case studies from journals, websites or industry sources.
- Assess actual and potential competitors and providers of 'alternatives' to your own venture to understand their strengths and vulnerabilities.
- Spend time in the market to learn about its environment and dynamics.
- Identify opportunities and plan how a venture could develop and exploit them: what strategy and resources would be most effective?

- Develop a business plan and get feedback on it from an objective, informed source (such as a qualified adviser).
- Contact and get to know potential investors such as 'business angels' to find out their investment criteria and how to present your proposition to them most effectively.

Marketing and Selling

- Get to know your market by visiting the customer and 'putting yourself in the shoes' of everyone concerned with your product or service, from the decision maker to the end user. Spending a couple of days a week with customers yields great understanding of the market as well as generating sales.
- Find out what is most important to the customer: why they buy, the important benefits and features to them, the marketing messages they pay attention to.
- Work with experienced marketing and sales professionals: learn what they do that is effective, why they do it and how it works for them.
- Get hands-on, sharp-end sales experience to learn the approaches to selling which work for you.
- Develop the skills needed to research a market, both face to face and in searching information sources.
- Develop an understanding of marketing methods, such as through professional marketing courses, and self-study through books and videos.

Financial Management

- Go on a short course to give you the basics in business finance.
- Get to know a business banker, an accountant and a financial adviser to find out their perspectives and 'tricks of the trade'.
- Prepare a financial plan and ask a financial professional to give you their objective critique.
- Learn to use the key ratios in managing the financial aspects[1] of any business venture, to understand the use of:
  - gross and net profit margins;
  - breakeven;
  - liquidity;
  - fixed and variable costs;
  - gearing;
  - return on capital, etc.
- Learn how to maximise cash flow, and what the fastest, surest ways are of getting cash in from customers, e.g. through prepayment and subscriptions.

---

1. These will be explored in the next book in the series *Dynamic Financial Management*.

Appendix 2

LIFE STORY TEMPLATE

My name: _____

Stage of my life:_____

What were my main activities during this stage of my life?

What were my significant experiences and learning episodes at this time?

What were my greatest successes?

What were my worst failures or mistakes?

What things were most important to me in what was I trying to achieve at this time?

What 'lessons did I learn'; the meanings and conclusions I drew from the key episodes?

In what ways was I enterprising during this time?

What capabilities and skills did I develop at this time?

What know-how and expertise did I develop at this time?

Appendix 3

OPPORTUNITY ASSESSMENT QUESTIONNAIRE

Use the questionnaire below to assess your opportunity.

- Answer the questions on each dimension.
- Where possible, use factual data to answer the questions.
- Total the scores for each dimension and plot these onto the scoring pentagon at the end of the questionnaire.
- Join the plotting points to show its profile.
- What does the profile suggest about the potential for exploiting this opportunity? Refer to Chapter 3 for interpretation.

Name or type of venture: _____

1. Investment

How much of your available financial assets does the venture require?	All.	5
	Above 75%.	4
	Above 50%.	3
	Above 25%.	2
	Below 25%.	1
	None.	0
How much of your available time, expertise and knowledge does the venture require?	All.	5
	Above 75%.	4
	Above 50%.	3
	Above 25%.	2
	Below 25%.	1
How much external financial investment is required as a percentage of the total funding required?	All.	5
	Above 75%.	4
	Above 50%.	3
	Above 25%.	2
	Up to 25%.	1
	None.	0
What investment of credibility is being made? (For example, through a recognised brand name, franchise, partnership ,joint venture or accreditation.)	Large amount.	5
	Significant.	4
	Moderate.	3
	Low.	2
	None.	0
Total points		

2. Risk

What proportion of the investment is secured on tangible assets with re-sale value?	All.	0
	Above 75%.	1
	Above 50%.	2
	Above 25%.	3
	Up to 25%.	4
	None.	5
Are all the essential elements on which the venture depends tested and proved to be predictable and reliable? (For example, consumer behaviour, process technology, suppliers?)	Completely untested.	5
	Largely untested.	4
	Partly unproven.	3
	Significantly proven.	2
	Completely predictable.	1
Do the people who will run the venture have proven skills, experience and track record in all its essential elements?	Few elements.	5
	Some elements.	4
	Most elements.	3
	All significant elements.	2
	All elements.	1
Have all the external factors, which could materially affect the venture, been identified and their potential impact assessed? (For example, economic factors, competitor behaviour.)	No analysis.	5
	Superficial analysis.	4
	Most factors analysed.	3
	All significant factors analysed	2
	Complete analysis of all factors.	1
Total points		

3. Return

What is the gross profit margin the venture is expected to make?	75-100%.	6
	50-74%.	5
	25-49%.	3
	10-24%.	2
	Less than 10%.	1
What is the anticipated return on investment each year?	100% plus	7
	75-99%.	6
	50-74%.	5
	25-49%.	3
	Less than 25%.	2
What is the anticipated growth in the value of the investment per year?	100% plus	7
	75-99%.	6
	50-74%.	5
	25-49%.	3
	Less than 25%.	2
Total Points		

4. Change

How does the venture create its market? (For example, by finding a new market, by identifying unmet demand, or by configuring customer requirements in a new way.)	A completely new market.	5
	An under developed market in which there is little competition.	4
	Extension of an existing market.	3
	Reconfigures customer requirements in a new way.	2
	An existing market.	1
Is the venture innovative? (For example, in creating a new product or in using new technology or production processes.)	Highly innovative.	5
	Significant innovation.	4
	Moderate innovation.	3
	Some innovation.	2
	Little innovation.	1
Does the venture use a new distribution method to sell to and to reach customers? (For example, how different will the customers' experience be from the current situation?)	Totally new.	5
	Significantly changed.	4
	Moderately changed.	3
	Little changed.	2
	Unchanged.	1
Will the venture lead to significant changes in the structure of the industry, e.g. for competitors and suppliers?	Radical change.	5
	Significant change.	4
	Moderate change.	3
	Little change.	2
	No change.	1
Total points		

5. Time

Will the project start?	Significantly in advance of competitors.	5
	Slightly in advance of competitors.	4
	At same time as competitors.	2
	Later than competitors.	1
How quickly will the project start to produce a return on the investment?	More than 2 years.	5
	1-2 years.	4
	6-12 months.	3
	3-6 months.	2
	Within 3 months.	1
For how long will the venture continue to produce a return on the investment?	Indefinitely.	5
	5- 10 years.	4
	2-5 years.	3
	1-2 years.	2
	Up to 1 year.	1
How likely is the project to create additional profitable opportunities during its lifespan? (For example, spin-offs, product extensions.)	Highly likely.	5
	Moderately likely.	3
	Unlikely.	1
Total points		

Scoring Pentagon

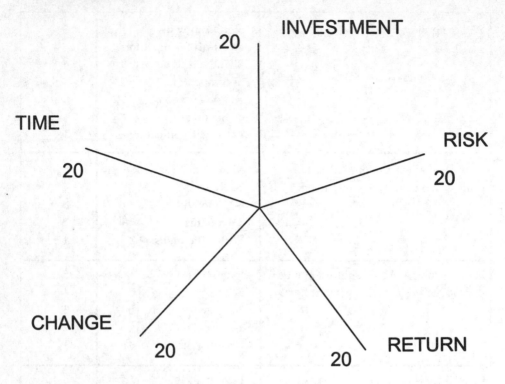

INTERPRETING THE PROFILE

Use the questions below to analyse the profile and consider ways in which the venture could be re-configured to improve its prospects.

- Is the profile aggressive? A large profile will show greater risk, higher reward, bigger investment, larger scale change and medium to longer timescales. This will require a high level of entrepreneurial management capability. Do you – or your team – possess this?

- Is the profile defensive? A tightly grouped profile will show lower degrees of investment, risk, reward, change and short to medium timescales. This may suggest an over-cautious approach, which will provide modest rewards. How can its potential be enhanced?

- Can the investment required be reduced, or more of it obtained from other investors?

- Is it an attractive investment? To what type of investor? Will you invest your money in it?

- What factors give rise to the degree of risk, and can any of these be reduced, e.g. through market or product testing, research, planning, finding people with the right experience?

- Is the projected return commensurate with the degree of risk?

- Does the degree of change in the venture increase its risk, and, if so, can this be reduced without detracting from the venture's competitive advantage?

- Can the venture achieve greater results through being more innovative?

- Can more value-adding spin-off services be created from the venture to enhance its earnings and lifetime?

- Can the timescales be altered, e.g. to bring forward the start of earnings, and to extend the earning lifetime of the venture?

- Can the value of the venture be increased over its lifetime?

CAREER PLAN FORMAT

What I want to achieve?

Goals and Motivations

- My personal vision for the future is:

- These are the values which are most important to me:

- These are my life goals for:

  - business

  - career

  - personal growth

  - family

  - social

Include when each goal is to be achieved and how success will be measured.

Increasing my personal value

- My value to myself and to others is based on:

- These are the ways in which I aim to build on my personal qualities to develop my career further:

Financial value   **by when**

- I aim to increase the value of my total net financial assets to:

- I aim to increase my annual financial income to:

How I will achieve my goals?

These are my plans for how I will achieve each of my goals:

Personal learning

- These are my goals for learning, through which I will be able to achieve my life goals:

Include in each plan, how you will gain the learning, by when, and who will help your learning.

Signed: _____   Date:_____

References and Select Bibliography

BOOKS

I Ansoff, *Corporate Strategy* (Harmondsworth: Penguin) 1987.

R Atkinson, *The Life Story Interview* (California: Sage) 1998.

A Bandura, *Social Foundations of Thought and Action: A Social Cognitive Theory* (New Jersey: Prentice-Hall) 1986.

S Birley & D Muzyka (eds), *Mastering Enterprise* (London: Financial Times/Pitman) 1997.

I Briggs Myers & M McCaulley, *Manual: A Guide to the Development and Use of the Myers-Briggs Type Indicator* (California: Consulting Psychologists Press) 1985.

D Deakins, *Entrepreneurship and Small Firms* (London: McGraw-Hill) 1996.

P Drucker, *Innovation and Entrepreneurship* (London: Heinemann) 1985.

R Gavron, M Cowling, G Holtham & A Westall, *The Entrepreneurial Society* (London: IPPR) 1998.

R Hebert & A Link, *The Entrepreneur: Mainstream Views and Radical Critiques* (New York: Praeger) 1988.

I Kirzner, *Competition and Entrepreneurship* (Chicago: The University of Chicago Press) 1973.

D Kolb, *Experiential Learning: Experience as the Source of Learning and Development* (New Jersey: Prentice-Hall) 1984.

L T C Rolt, *Isambard Kingdom Brunel* (Harmondsworth: Pelican) 1970.

J Schumpeter, *The Theory of Economic Development* (Harvard: Harvard University Press) 1934.

D Storey, *Understanding the Small Business Sector* (London: Routledge) 1994.

K Vesper, *New Venture Strategies* (New Jersey: Prentice-Hall) 1980.

S Vyakarnam & J Leppard, *A Marketing Action Plan for the Growing Business* (London: Kogan Page) 1995.

P Wickham, *Strategic Entrepreneurship* (London: Pitman) 1997.

S Williams, *Lloyd's Bank Small Business Guide* (Harmondsworth: Penguin) 1998.

T Watson & P Harris, *The Emergent Manager* (London: Sage) 1999.

ACADEMIC JOURNALS

B Bird, "Implementing Entrepreneurial Ideas: The Case for Intention" *Academy of Management Review* (1988) Vol. 13, No. 3, pp. 442-453.

N Boyd & G Vozikis, "The Influence of Self-efficacy on the Development of Entrepreneurial Intentions and Actions" *Entrepreneurship Theory & Practice* (1994) Vol. 18, No. 4, pp. 63-77.

D Deakins & M Freel, "Entrepreneurial Learning and the Growth Process in SMEs" *The Learning Organisation*, MCB University Press (1998) Vol. 5, No. 3, pp. 144-155.

W Gartner, "'Who is an Entrepreneneur?' is the Wrong Question" *Entrepreneurship Theory & Practice* (1989) Vol. 13, No. 4, pp. 47-67.

A Gibb, "The Enterprise Culture and Education" *Entrepreneurship Theory & Practice* (1993) Vol. 11, No. 3, pp. 11-34.

W Gibb Dyer Jr, "Toward a Theory of Entrepreneurial Careers" *Entrepreneurship Theory & Practice* (1994) Vol. 19, No. 2, pp. 7-21.

R Mitchell, "Oral History and Expert Scripts: Demystifying the Entrepreneurial Experience" *Int. Journal of Entrepreneurial Behaviour & Research* (1997) Vol. 3, No. 2, pp. 122-139.

D Mitton, "Entrepreneurship: One More Time – Non-cognitive Characteristics that make the Cognitive Clock Tick" *Frontiers of Entrepreneurship Research*, Babson (1997) pp. 188-203.

R Reuber & E Fischer, "The Learning Experiences of Entrepreneurs" *Frontiers of Entrepreneurship Research*, Babson (1993) pp. 234-245.

J Young & D Sexton, "Entrepreneurial Learning: A Conceptual Framework" *Journal of Enterprising Culture* (1997) Vol. 5, No. 3, pp. 223-248.

T Watson, "Entrepreneurship and Professional Management: A Fatal Distinction" *International Small Business Journal* (1995) Vol. 13, No. 2, pp. 34-46.

INDEX

Dynamic Financial Management
for Sure Business Growth

Ian Marshall

If there is one area which consistently bemuses people in the small, growing business sector it is the area of finance. Failure rates for those embarking on the highly dangerous, and often to them, unchartered waters of enterprise, are still unacceptably high. Yet a little basic knowledge can actually help those embarking on the voyage not only survive, but prosper.

The latest in a series of new, original, cutting-edge books produced by Blackhall Publishing in association with the BDO Stoy Hayward Centre for Growing Businesses at Nottingham Business School, *Dynamic Financial Management* focuses on helping the reader gain an understanding of the fundamental concepts of dynamic, as opposed to static, financial control. The author, Ian Marshall, argues that the overall profitability of a business is determined by just three factors: cost, price and volume. A thorough understanding of how these factors interrelate will go a long way towards understanding how to manage the finances of a company. In a time of rapidly changing economic conditions, on a global scale, the book provides a reliable methodology and a sound basis for assessing the viability of the different strategic options open to an organisation in this area.

The book draws on case studies which provide practical examples of the dangers faced by either a newly-formed business, an established business contemplating expansion, or a business focusing on survival. The measures recommended highlight the relationship between growth and financial stability. The book explains the key dynamic measures of financial performance that address the future rather than the past and provides a practical and readable analysis of the vital issues involved in a true understanding of business finance. It will be of vital benefit to practising businessmen, and to students participating in entrepreneurship or business management programmes at either undergraduate or post-graduate level.

The Author
Ian Marshall is the former head of the Business Development Centre at Nottingham Business School.

220 pages
1-901657-88-4 £17.99 pbk: October 1999

The Growing Business Series

Growing a business, after the initial start-up period, is a difficult thing to do. It is fraught with danger, and requires coping with a set of unique, and at times, competing demands.

Ideas need to be turned into practice, a mission statement and a vision need to be defined and implemented, strategies and tactics have to be developed, and complex subjects, such as finance and people management, have to be dealt with.

The Growing Business Series is based on the leading-edge, original research being carried out at The Centre for Growing Businesses at Nottingham Business School, into entrepreneurship and business growth. The philosophy underpinning the series is that the skills necessary to start and develop a business can be learnt and are not hereditary. Growth is dependent upon entrepreneurship, and also on an understanding of the fundamentals of business management. This series provides that understanding.

Forthcoming titles in *The Growing Business Series*:

Marshall: *Dynamic Financial Management for Sure Business Growth*   Rae: People Management in the Growing Business
Vyakarnam: *Planning for Growth*

For further details on the series please contact
Tony Mason at Blackhall Publishing.

The above books can be purchased at any good
bookshop or direct from:
BLACKHALL PUBLISHING
26 Eustace Street
Dublin 2.

Telephone: +353 (0)1-677-3242;
Fax: +353 (0)1-677-3243;
e-mail: blackhall@tinet.ie

Coventry University